PS-CQC-211

D0122885

Revival That Reforms

Other books by Bill Hull

The Disciple-Making Pastor
The Disciple-Making Church
New Century Disciple Making
Seven Steps to Transform Your Church
Building High Commitment in a Low-Commitment
   World

Revival That Reforms

Making It Last

Bill Hull

Fleming H. Revell
A Division of Baker Book House
Grand Rapids, Michigan 49516

© 1998 by Bill Hull

Published by Fleming H. Revell
a division of Baker Book House Company
P.O. Box 6287, Grand Rapids, MI 49516-6287

Printed in the United States of America

All rights reserved. No part of this publication may be reproduced, stored in a retrieval system, or transmitted in any form or by any means—for example, electronic, photocopy, recording—without the prior written permission of the publisher. The only exception is brief quotations in printed reviews.

Library of Congress Cataloging-in-Publication Data

Hull, Bill, 1946–
    Revival that reforms : making it last / Bill Hull.
       p. cm.
    Includes bibliographical references
    ISBN 0-8007-1752-X (cloth)
    1. Revivals. 2. Pastoral theology. 3. Church. 4. Commitment to the church.
  5. Mission of the church. I. Title.
BV3793.H85 1998
269'.2—dc21   98-9841

Scripture quotations are taken from the HOLY BIBLE, NEW INTERNATIONAL VERSION®. NIV®. Copyright © 1973, 1978, 1984 by International Bible Society. Used by permission of Zondervan Publishing House. All rights reserved.

For current information about all releases from Baker Book House, visit our web site:
http://www.bakerbooks.com

Warning sign on the ruins
of an ancient British Church:

"Anyone damaging these ruins
will be prosecuted."

George Will

Contents

Introduction   9

Part One Revival

1. What Is Revival?   15
2. Do We Need Revival?   35
3. Breakthroughs   43
4. Barriers   53
5. The Nature of Revival   87

Part Two Reformation

6. The Starting Line   109
7. Redefine the Mission   115
8. Redesign Your Infrastructure   171
9. Reassign Personnel   207

Appendix A: New Life Church Philosophy
    of Ministry   221
Appendix B: Purpose, Philosophy,
    and Principles   223
Appendix C: Sample Church Plan   231
Notes   237

Introduction

There I sat, one of forty-two thousand clergy gathered in the Georgia Dome at the Promise Keepers Clergy Conference, for the purpose of meeting God. Many of us had been directly pressured to go by laymen. Others had received inferences that not to go was a venial sin. The strong undercurrent was (and I believe it was largely true) that God was giving his gatekeepers an opportunity to get in on what he was doing before he was forced to "wire around the institutional church" to complete the church's mission.

Some of us came expectantly, thinking this event could break the dam of rebellion, divisions, and racism among Christians. God would pour out his Spirit. Let the REVIVAL begin.

To some, renewal or revival meant shedding tears, lifting hands, or running in circles around the floor of the arena. It could be anything from exorcising evil spirits to casting out old hymnals. Whatever revival is, we were all for it. We also widely believed that once it happened, the church would be radically changed for the good. So we waited and prayed for the mysterious move of God.

Midmorning on the second day, the dam of resistance sprung a big leak and God's healing water poured over his servants' dry spirits. Cynicism was jettisoned through a hole in the dome that later miraculously closed. By the time we left, we had met with God. Thousands of pastors with strengthened backs and set jaws, declared, "I won't give up.

I'm going home and give it my best. I want to be a carrier of the real disease in order to infect others."

But a strong sense of sadness descended on me in the midst of the rejoicing and the laughter. Reality took a big bite out of my optimism. *The same problems that so many pastors left at home that contributed to their discouragement and disappointment were waiting for them on their return.* Many faithful servants are not fruitful, and they know it. Many churches bear little fruit and don't stop their banal robotics long enough to notice. God has called us to be both faithful and fruitful.

Every church leader longs to experience the biblical descriptions of God's empowering and multiplying his people. So thousands went home with renewed vision and determination. Now, eighteen months later, many of those leaders are again discouraged and disappointed because whatever happened at that conference wasn't enough to really change their pastoral behavior or their church's effectiveness.

Events create impact; they motivate and give reasons to commit; but they rarely transform behavior in a lasting way. Events can stir the stagnated and refresh the stale; meetings can help build momentum and provide the inspiration needed to give people hope. They can leave an impression, but that does not necessarily lead to lasting change or transformation. Lasting change is internal and it requires a process in order to become transformation. *Therein lies the reason that the church is not prepared for spiritual awakening and why when it comes, we will be poor stewards of it. We are easily IMPRESSED, BUT NOT TRANSFORMED.*

One of the great humiliations of the church is that nearly every great revival has originated outside the church. The church is usually weighed down with its own responsibility and can't seem to dig out of itself to prepare for awakening. For the church, revival means humiliation, a bitter knowledge of unworthiness, and an open confession of sin.

Thesis: **If spiritual awakening is to come to the church, it will require both revival and reformation.**

10

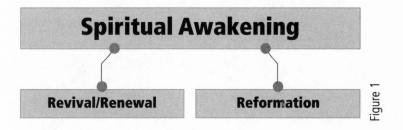

Figure 1

So much of God's work of energizing his church has been wasted because we have pursued revival without its corresponding partner, reformation. Revival is the starting line, not the finish line. After revival begins, the real work starts. Revival brings power; reformation transforms that power into lasting change. We need to go beyond the inspiration of the moment, beyond the event mentality, beyond conventional thinking to find a process that will lead to lasting change.

PART ONE
Revival

What Is Revival?   1

I gathered with 150 other leaders in a very fine hotel to consider how to reach America for Christ. My discussion group focused on what elements and actions were needed. As the hours passed, a consistent theme developed: "Unless God sends a revival, there is no way that our country will be rescued, and our efforts will be in vain." Many viewed revival as some sort of fetish that would erase the troubling issues confronting us. God would suspend normal operations to inject his church in particular and society in general with power and truth.

I found the direction of the discussion troubling for two reasons. The first was the sense of passive resignation to ineffectiveness without the special sovereign act of God. The second was, What about all that stuff already in the Bible—the promises of power to obey and fruitfulness to those who abide in Christ?

I raised my hand and entered into treacherous territory when I said, "We are talking as if we have no real chance to reach America unless God sends revival. I am for revival but I am not sure what we mean by it. Are we really helpless without it?" There was general consensus that God sends revival in his good time and according to his plan and that prayer, unity, and the consultations and summits are efforts of the church to prepare itself for revival.

I then asked, "What if God determines that he will send revival in 2017? What happens in the meantime?" This surfaced questions: What exactly do we mean by revival? If it comes, what difference would it make?

Most revival talk reminds me of our two-week revivals at the Northside Pilgrim Holiness Church at 46th and Kingsley Drive in Indianapolis, Indiana. It was always interesting to me that we knew exactly when God would revive us, because we scheduled it for two weeks in the fall and then again in the spring. During revivals we met every evening and twice on Sunday. If God really blessed, it could go on for weeks. As a ten-year-old I fervently prayed that God would not bless. It wasn't that we had TV or anything like that. It was that I already knew I was going to hell and didn't like to be reminded every night.

I could never forget the night that the evangelist started walking down the middle aisle with a huge black Bible in one hand and a "sweat rag" in the other. He stopped at my row and walked toward me. Somebody had "tipped him off." He said, "Billy, do you want to go to the altar?" "Sure," I sputtered, and off I went, surrounded by a lot of old people.

You see the rule was that we couldn't close the service till something happened, so I was trying to move things along. I prayed earnestly and was assured that I had been saved. I even felt saved until recess the next day when I called a classmate a dirty name and hit him in the mouth. A week later I was the same; two months later, our church was the same. All this revival stuff just seemed to be a lot of activity without lasting significance.

I have opportunity to speak to a variety of church leaders from various theological viewpoints. One subject I speak on is spiritual awakening. A third of the time I am asked not to mention revival, because either the group I'm speaking to doesn't believe in it, or there is strong disagreement as to its importance or what it is.

Revival is not a biblical word or concept per se.

This kind of confusion among the general Christian populace and Christian leaders leads to every response from passive resignation to active skepticism. So first we need to consider the question, What is revival?

What Is Revival?

Revival is not a biblical word or concept per se. The word is thrown around as if we all know what it means. There is a consensus across the theological spectrum that revival means to fully experience the fulfillment of both the Great Commandment and the Great Commission, but expectations and descriptions of the revival manifestations vary greatly. Televangelists normally see it differently than parish priests. So what are the issues?

Biblical Perspective

Linguistic Considerations

Most argument begins with linguistic considerations. I will leave the real theological work on this subject to the real theologians. My purpose is to take note of the obvious: The word *revival* and what we have made of it cannot, as such, be found in Scripture.

17

The Old Testament employs the causative construction in Hebrew translated "live" or "to come to life" (1 Kings 17:22; Job 33:4; Ezek. 37:5, 6, 14). These verses speak of the Spirit of God causing something to come to life. This form of cause-and-effect language is used 250 times in the Old Testament. It may be translated "revive," "restore," "preserve," "heal," "prosper," or "flourish."[1] The concept of people being renewed is clearly present in the history of Israel and with the people of God. But there is a clear difference between how Scripture speaks about it and how historians describe major awakenings. Historical theology is developed differently than systematic or biblical theology.

It is dangerous to give the variety of spiritual experiences in Scripture one label, namely revival, and then canonize it as the only hope for the church, the nation, and all of humankind.

The New Testament is a bit more straightforward. To "live again" refers to the raising of a son (Luke 15:24) or to employ a spiritual gift (2 Tim. 1:5–6). Of course the concept of "becoming born again" (John 3:3) is one of the kaleidoscope of terms used in the New Testament to describe regeneration.

Scripture's immediate revelation is that the imparting and reviving of supernatural spiritual life is pervasive. *Revival* is simply a term we have given to special activity of God throughout history.

Observational Theology

Major events in both Old and New Testaments that restored God's people as a class and individuals could be considered works of renewal or revival. The continuous renewing of Abraham, Isaac, and particularly Moses are wonderful examples of God's mercy and willingness to restore his people. Cases of Israel's renewal are plenteous, whether it be various lessons during a forty-year trek through the wilderness that should have taken six weeks or the resurgence built around one of the five major feasts instituted by God to help his people remember his faithfulness. Examples of revival experiences include the cleansing of Israel during the life of Josiah or under the influence of the leadership of Ezra and Nehemiah. God sent one prophet after another to deliver his promises for both good and ill. The invitation is ever extended: "If my people, who are called by my name, will humble themselves and pray and seek my face and turn from their wicked ways, then will I hear from heaven and will forgive their sin and will heal their land" (2 Chron. 7:14).

The fact that people were revived when in contact with Jesus dominates the theologically gray areas that cover the transition from Judaism to Christianity. The calling of Matthew, raising of the dead, restoring sight to the blind, giving able legs to the lame, and reclaiming Peter after his failings are all signposts and encouragement to every seeker.

Jesus laid out his mission of reviving humankind: "The Spirit of the Lord is on me, because he has anointed me to preach good news to the poor. He has sent me to proclaim freedom for the prisoners and recovery of sight for the blind, to release the oppressed, to proclaim the year of the Lord's favor" (Luke 4:18–19).

Spiritual revival is in the Bible. Being radically transformed by the power of God based on the finished work of the resurrected Christ is in the Bible. Whatever it is called, revived, renewed, refreshed, regenerated, liberated, empowered, filled, raised, or healed, I'm for it!

It is dangerous to give the variety of spiritual experiences in Scripture one label, namely revival, and then canonize it as the only hope for the church, the nation, and all of humankind. This leads to reliance on God to do all the work—not only his but ours.

All spiritual work is God's work, I know that, but Jesus left over two hundred commands for his church. Our desperation for revival as a solution is in part evidence of our failure to walk daily in the power of the Spirit and to obey what God has already paid for and equipped us to do. He expects us to accomplish it. Looking for a way out through revival is very much like a young person who makes a series of bad financial decisions that immerse him in bad debt and then begs his parents or friends to bail him out. It is not more spiritual to focus efforts on prayer and fasting and seeking God than to go out and obey God in the power he has already provided.

People do not get more power to do God's will in revival than in normal times. If it takes only the faith that is the size of a mustard seed to move a mountain, "more faith" is a misnomer. Christians need only to apply a necessary amount of faith to a certain task. We call it "more faith" or "great faith" when the task seems larger to us. The fact is that one thing is just as easy as another for God. This is why Jesus asked the question of skeptics, "Which is harder to say, your sins are forgiven or take up your bed and walk?" For God they are the same. We don't need more power, we need to apply the power God has already provided.

In revival times what works to inspire one person becomes widespread and sweeps through the church like wildfire. There seems to be more power because more people experience the same thing, and there is a synergy or "critical mass" that explodes so that it is noticed by many and recorded as a special move of God. But the amount of power required is always the same.

Iain Murray both clarifies and defines the nature of revival.

> What happens in revivals is not to be seen as something miraculously different from the regular experience of the church. The difference lies in degree, not in kind. In an outpouring of the Spirit spiritual influence is more widespread, convictions are deeper, and feelings more intense, but all this is only a heightening of normal Christianity.[2]

How much power does it take not to lie or to stay faithful to one's spouse? Is God's power like gasoline? When we move up a steep grade of resisting the temptation not to be faithful to our spouse, do we use more fuel than when we resist the temptation to put inaccurate information on a credit application? The same issue arises in what it means to be filled with the Spirit. Being filled does not mean that we weigh more because we get several ounces of the Spirit that fill our spirits to the brim. This issue illustrates the limits of language. "Being filled" is simply a matter of the will and who is in control of our attitudes and actions at any given moment.

Historical Perspective

It is no surprise that history has much more to say about revival than Scripture does. If we could return all the literature on revival to its original form, we could create a considerable forest. Richard Owen Roberts's annotated bibliography on revival contains 5,983 titles. The majority focus (and rightly so) on the First and Second Great Awakenings. The First Great Awakening, which took place in the early 1700s, was the experiential application of the reformation orthodoxy. The Second Great Awakening started in the early 1800s and it expanded world missionary witness and launched many impressive programs of social reform, including the abolition of slavery. The reason these awakenings are called "great" is that both led to widespread cultural renewal and their duration was at least thirty years. Both impacted Great Britain and America.

People do not get more power to do God's will in revival than in normal times.

The first British version is primarily attributed to John Wesley, even though Wesley reaped more benefits than being its progenitor. A good word should also be said for Count Ludwig von Zinzendorf, who lived during the same period on the European continent. He gave Pietism good leadership and established *Herrnhut,* "the Lord's watch," a community of accountability and spiritual direction. In America Jonathan Edwards inherited his grandfather's parish in 1727. He characterized it as "dry bones" and said, "They shuffled doctrines aimlessly like a faded deck of cards."[3]

It would be fair to propose that Jonathan Edwards was one of the most godly men and perhaps the greatest intellect ever produced in America. He wrote the now famous *Distinguishing Marks of a Work of the Holy Spirit* as an apologetic to answer attacks from fellow pastors. The awakening reached its peak in 1740 and it continued to impact America until 1770.

Under Edwards's leadership revival took on a distinctive theological characteristic. Until 1830 one single definition of the phenomenon prevailed.

> A revival was a sovereign and large giving of the Spirit of God, resulting in the addition of many to the Kingdom of God. Such was the definition of Edwards. Though the word revival does not appear to have been used in print before Cotton Mather's *Magnalia Christi Americana* of 1702, the phenomenon was understood in the same way long before that date.[4]

In other words, revival was what they called God manifesting his glory. In the process there would be increased awareness of sin and the holiness of God, a widespread repentance, and conversions at a greatly accelerated rate. It was not something man could bring on, manufacture, or in any way control. *The focus was not on people; it was on God himself. Revival was defined as the extraordinary and not the normal condition of the church.*

The Second Wave

At the start of the 1800s there was a second major surge of power and renewal again in both England and the United States. This move of God was different from that in the First Great Awakening in both its theological bent and in who took it to the people. The First Great Awakening's theology was focused on the sovereign action of God; this second move started to take on a more pragmatic and activist theology. The first awakening's prophets were men of great intellectual "firepower," like Edwards, while the second was dominated by circuit-riding evangelists and teachers, both Baptists and Methodists. As Richard Lovelace notes, "They were not always well educated; their theology and practice were often open to question. But they had the courage and calling to go where the frontier was developing and they spoke the people's language."[5] This awakening also led to more practical applications and birthed many new social and missionary organizations.

While both awakenings were attended by trained theologians—men who had mastered their culture—the second depended on the leadership of lay evangelists like Charles Finney, D. L. Moody, and Billy Sunday. It also led, writes Lovelace:

> to progressively shallower spirituality among evangelicals and to a loss of intellectual command. This loss of intellectual mastery proved to be a critical weakness, since the secular humanist world view which had been in the process of construction since the Enlightenment was receiving powerful reinforcement from the contributions of Darwin, Marx and Freud.[6]

A Different View of Revival

Remember, before 1830 one view of revival dominated the church's thinking. As early as 1832 Calvin Colton proposed a theory that genuine revivals could be classified into two different types, the old and the new. The old are those that come mysteriously and unexpectedly, directly from the presence of the Lord. You would wait for them like men wait for showers of rain.[7]

The new form of revival is associated with Charles Finney, who took the lead and championed an entirely different paradigm. Finney taught that man could take actions that would lead to a sure revival. Revival could be secured by the fulfillment of prerequisites; therefore, revival should be the norm. It could be permanent. Colton and Finney, along with their followers, considered the older forms of revival no longer needed. Some new techniques were designed to make revival meetings protracted in nature. Added to that was the management of such events, with the anxious seat (where people could be prayed over or witnessed to), long invitations, and intentionally raising the emotional state of attendees to get visible results. This led J. H. Rice to write,

We should not become evangelistic concerning what manifestations we want to see as proof of God at work.

"From the little that I saw, I would say that if good is done by these irregular means, it is done at frightening expense. It is like slaying hundreds to save one."[8] Some present-day methods are guilty of the same abuse.

I have attended meetings where the sponsors needed to see some results so they could justify the time and money expended. I don't mean this cynically, but an entire genre of the church measures God's presence by outward manifestation.

It is difficult to determine how much difference such manifestations really make. When people are preconditioned by their subculture to respond a certain way, the outward action may simply express "their way" of responding to God in that church. People with their hands thrust heavenward and crying or laughing may be the exact same thing as other Christians in another place quietly kneeling and whispering, "Thank you, Lord."

One outward expression is not better or worse than another. The issue is inward reality. Does outward expression lead to right living, right thinking; does it change lives? You can kneel, sing, or cry for hours; the only thing that counts is what happens when you exit the sanctuary and start living. Each expression has its acceptable forum. We should not become evangelistic concerning what manifestations we want to see as proof of God at work.

Colton, along with others, later abandoned the idea that by taking specific actions man could bring on a revival. Finney, however, held fast to his beliefs because of the evidence. He claimed that events, such as the Fulton Street prayer meetings, were proof of his beliefs, but people who were involved denied that any lasting revival took place. Despite the work of many revivalists from the 1830s onward, spiritual awakening did not continue. And in fact many of the continued revivals, which Finney's methods allegedly started, diffused quickly.

"So why is this important?" one might ask. If Finney was right and we can get a revival by doing the right seven things, then to live in any other state than perpetual revival is sin.[9] So we are to believe that what God did in the First and Second Great Awakenings is normal; what remains of the last one hundred years is abnormal, below God's standard, and a powerful combination of individual, corporate, and cultural sin. As James McLoughlin writes, "If Finney's theology was correct then there was not a choice but between feast or famine in religion."[10] Finney would say it should always be feasting time. The reality of both human nature and the teaching of the Bible marches right over this wishful thinking. The reality of the flesh requires special moves of God in order to compensate for our slow but sure slide into spiritual corruption.

The Special Is Normal

Finney's kind of thinking requires that we all live on an emotional level akin to the mountaintop experience. Under such a belief anything other than optimum performance is evidence that God has withdrawn his blessing. Not living in revival indicates that God's Spirit is not dwelling and working in the church all the time.

The Spirit of God was given to the church forever (John 14:16). God is at work in the church "according to the plan of him who works out everything in conformity with the purpose of his will" (Eph. 1:11). The believer actually walks in fellowship with God while responding to the ministry of the Holy Spirit in the midst of struggling with sin (1 John 1:7–9).

"So I say, live by the Spirit, and you will not gratify the desires of the sinful nature. For the sinful nature desires what is contrary to the Spirit, and the Spirit what is contrary to the sinful nature. They are in conflict with each other, so that you do not do what you want" (Gal. 5:16–17). Scripture is clear that the "flesh," or as the NIV translates it "sinful nature," does not improve. We have the potential to live victorious lives, but we are not promised nor should we expect to live sinlessly. What makes revival or renewal special is that there is a normal. That normal should and can be walking in the Spirit, obeying God, and bearing fruit. Again it comes back to the *degree* of what God is doing rather than the *kind* of thing God is doing. There can be real improvement without revival. A slow and gradual growth is normal for the church. Spiritual development is a process, not an event.

Contemporary Finney

Finney's impact on present culture shows in our addiction to big events. The church around the world, but more so in America, depends on large meetings with major personalities and a good show. We measure success by how many were there and who was there. We hold meetings that are meant to bring on revival, that make things happen, stimulating conversions or church growth. I doubt that most leaders believe that we can, by assembling, pray or call heaven down on demand. There is a sense, however, in which we would rather attend gatherings than slug it out in the trenches.

This does not mean we should not gather for prayer and fasting. I do not advocate that we stop holding evangelistic events and conferences on how to strengthen our lives and our churches. However, I do warn against expecting God to bring to life a preconditioned, culturally colored image of what some people would call revival. Many articles and sermons indicate that if only we would pray longer and cry out louder, God would have to act now and in a big way. *This is the trap—that revival depends on us, that if we just try harder, God will do something the way we think he should.* We should pray; we should fast; we should also follow directions and continue in what he already has provided. This is not either/or; it is a matter of perspective and emphasis.

Is There a Middle?

Can we find a balance between the *sola sovereignty* position (prepare and wait) and the *sola seeker* position (God waits until we act)? I find no virtue in always being half right or half wrong, thus the middle may be the wrong goal. It reminds me of Søren Kierkegaard's observation, "When everybody is a Christian, nobody is a Christian."[11] By making everyone right, all important distinctives are vaporized under the guise of tolerance. And as G. K. Chesterton said, "tolerance is for those who have no convictions."

The solution is to take refuge in humility and mystery. I take comfort in the knowledge that my role is to prepare myself for God's actions, knowing that he has promised to answer prayer and sustain his church. I humble myself before God by praying, seeking, obeying, and longing for his more direct action on my life, the church, and general culture (1 Peter 5:5–7).

I also rest in the mystery of his will (Eph. 1:7–10). I have very little certitude as to why God has sent revival so infrequently. But I am sure, although the church is racked with a variety of sins and pathologies, the reason is not the church alone. I find it very comfortable to seek God for the sake of knowing him more fully and to accept his better plan. So the church should fully seek God and all that he wills to do for us and through us. It would be wrong to sit back and be laissez-faire or to promote seeking God just to see revival. The point of seeking God is relationship; it is pursuing God for the pleasure of knowing our Creator. The completion of mission is the happy by-product.

One Word—Different Perceptions

The term *revival* is loaded down with cultural and stereotypical baggage. The Builder generation (born before 1946) love the word, Boomers (1946–1964) tolerate it, Busters (1965–1979) don't use it, and we have yet to figure out what Gen Xers (1980 to present) think about it.

This varying response is the fate of religious words that are slung about without precision. For Builders it often means college students cleaning up their lives and even their rooms and the closing of classes for several days. For such people, when scheduled meetings go four weeks instead of two, revival is transformed from lowercase to UPPERCASE!

Purists reserve the word for an extended expression of God at work, as documented in historical writings. The truth is, however, that no one really knows what revival is. Because it is not a biblical word or concept, anyone can put this manufactured label on anything that looks like a positive, God-related force. Various prayer summits, conferences, and concerts give people an emotional taste of what revival might be like.

When a friend of mine recently won an award for a book, he was presented with a medallion and subsequently a large roll of adhesive medallions to place on his books. He was having fun handing out the medallions so friends could stick them on anything they liked. In the spirit of jocularity I stuck a few on my books, and a few other less "holy" objects. Likewise we may feel tempted to stick a *revival* label on whatever we want to champion. Because of its amorphous nature, a word like *revival* lends itself to great abuse and confusion.

Iain Murray comments: "It may be argued that any attempt to define revival is pointless for the word itself is not scriptural and indeed as J. W. Alexander says 'may not be wisely chosen.' But rightly or wrongly, it was chosen and its sense was commonly recognized over a long period of time."[12]

It seems as if we are stuck with the word, so we are to make the best of it.

What Actually Happens?

I would like to reposition revival, make it culturally palatable by stripping it of its cultural baggage and describing what it actually does. It is not so much the positive work of God that troubles Christians and outsiders; it is the negative images and the view by some evangelicals that it violates their theology. It is a virtue that some have set aside partisan theology to assign revival, whatever it is, to the largest branch of theology: mystery.

Because I am not a theologian, I will not attempt to inter-act with the existing reams of literature. Because I am not a historian, I will not survey all revival dynamics. I am a the-ological pragmatist. I am interested in sorting out what actu-ally happens so others like me can better understand the nature of God at work. There are many good works on this subject. I have chosen to rely on what respected thinkers say happens.

Awakening Christians

J. I. Packer defines revival as "a work of God by his Spirit through his word bringing the spiritually dead to living faith in Christ and renewing the inner life of Christians who have grown slack and sleepy."[13] Packer goes on to say, "Revival thus animates or re-animates churches and Christian groups to make a spiritual and moral impact on communities. It comprises an initial reviving, followed by a maintained state of revivedness."[14] He says the marks of genuine revival are:

1. Awesome sense of the presence of God and the truth of the gospel.
2. Profound awareness of sin, leading to repentance.
3. A heartfelt embrace of the glorified, loving, pardon-ing Christ.
4. An intensifying and speeding up of the work of grace.
5. Many conversions.
6. Personal revival takes place in context of community movement.

Jonathan Edwards is considered the leading thinker of his time and a person of impeccable credentials concerning what happens in revival. J. I. Packer points out three pri-mary teachings of Edwards on revival.

1. Revival is an extraordinary work of God the Holy Spirit reinvigorating and propagating Christian piety in a community.

29

2. Revivals have a central place in the revealed purposes of God.
3. Revivals are the most glorious of all God's works in the world.[15]

Edwards's first teaching lines up with virtually all opinion both studied and subjective as to the nature of revival. The second teaching—centrality to the purposes of God—indicates that God acts with a certain timing as it relates to the church's redemptive mission. When the church is weak, outreach is failing, and the sending base has begun to erode, one could reasonably conclude that via prayer and concerted seeking of God, that the church is ripe for revival.

Edwards's idea that the most glorious aspect of God's work is revival comes from his belief that the conversion of one soul was more magnificent than the creation itself. I suppose the rationale is that during revival more souls are converted, so revival must be the most glorious state of all for the church. It logically follows, as Edwards believed, that Christians have a duty to pray for revival.

Dimensions of Revival

Christians prayed and saw a special sweep of God at the Brownsville Assembly of God Church in Pensacola, Florida. It began on Father's Day, 1995, and since then more than fifty-six thousand people have indicated that they have made commitments to Christ.

Two years before the outbreak of revival the pastor called on the church to pray. On Sunday nights they would set up twelve banners that identified the needs of the congregation. People would gather around them and pray. Then they invited in evangelists that God was using and it all started.

On Father's Day the pastor felt a strong current of power run through his body. People started coming forward and they were there all day until 4:00 P.M. They started again at 6:00 P.M. and continued until 1:00 A.M. The revival has been the vehicle for thousands of conversions and the church has reaped eight hundred new members, along with revitalized ministries.

This is what Edwards was describing: People longing to be revived and uniting in prayer to ask for a great harvest of souls. This is indeed, the greatest miracle. However, this great work touched only a small segment of the church.

Sociologist Os Guinness believes a national awakening would require more dimensions. A true revival would need to:

- widely penetrate culture and generate new public policy
- address various levels of cultural authority
- have theological depth and coherence, not just spiritual devotion
- have intellectual firepower; theologians would need to weigh in on this issue
- have a moral passion to transform people and the vision to reform churches and evangelism
- have the intellectual character to bring substantial ideas to public life and discourse
- rise above shallow revivalism and revive revival itself
- impact belief and behavior, determining what churches do with their resources and what individuals do as citizens[16]

This would bring integrity to the Christian worldview, rather than swallowing various political philosophies of the major parties.

After reading stacks of books, reviewing many articles, listening to sermons, and conversing with people who care deeply about revival, I've found that a few common themes emerge.

1. Periodically God takes special action by sending extra power and blessing to his church. This is good and

31

desirable, and all serious Christians long for it and pray for it.

2. Generally this action is preceded by the church's seeking God in special times of prayer, heartfelt repentance, and an acute awareness of sin.

3. When God sends his extra power, it leads, to a larger degree than is usual, to repentance, conversions, and interest in the Bible, the church, and its mission.

4. The church community comes to life, and there is a renewed sense of the presence of God and the urgency of mission.

5. God's action is intentional in its timing and moves the redemptive agenda forward.

6. God receives greater glory in revival than at any other time because there is clear understanding that only God could initiate what is happening.

7. The impact of God's special work spreads to all of the culture. It influences politics and society's various institutions. It lifts the morality of culture both in discourse and behavior.

8. Its length and depth depend largely on the preparedness of the church to be good stewards of what God has sent.

Degree, not kind, as Murray pointed out in his description of revival, is the key to understanding what is happening and what is not happening. This helps clear the fog that covers this mysterious work of God, since God's special work is just more of God's normal work.

There are a few things that it should be said that revival is clearly *not*.

Revival Is NOT God Suspending the Rules

The way people talk about revival, it sounds as if God suspends his rules while he rolls over his church with an irresistible wave of his Spirit and power. Many who make such claims remind me of the hapless people who expect their proverbial "ship to come in." We normally criticize such people for not doing the normal things that are required to be successful to hammer out a living. But many well-meaning Christians think that when God does his special work, it will retroactively correct what has and has not been done in the past.

Thinking that we won't have to repent, walk daily in the Spirit, confront wrenching decisions, wrestle with temptation, read Scripture, pray, give money to God by faith, and so on denies his words to us. Whatever God does, he will not violate what he has already revealed in Scripture. Each of us can experience complete renewal based on what he has already provided and promised.

Revival Is NOT the Machinery of Revivalism

The negative transition took place in the middle 1800s, when the old, comprehensive concept of revival, extolling the manifestation of the glory of God, was replaced by the post-Finneyan machinery of revivalism. Holding a revival became synonymous with using new methods to do mass evangelism. This reached its most garish zenith in the middle 1900s, with the local church scheduling two-week revivals with the evangelists, the song leader, the soloist, and the children's worker. Revivalism was the forerunner to the modern church-growth movement.

I would define revivalism as man's best effort to stimulate what God alone can accomplish, true revival. There is really nothing wrong with the church's efforts to stimulate and grow the church. Working to make progress on the Great Commission is not only honorable but a command. The combined effort of the church in obeying God can lead to a synergy that could prepare the church for revival. But assigning the term *revival* to various crusades, conferences, and seminars on church-growth principles breeds confusion.

Revival Is NOT Just a Repeat of What Has Happened Before

This has become known as the antiquarian fallacy. If we form a concept of revival for the future based on a particu-

33

lar revival of the past, that pattern becomes a norm or measure and exposes us to various dangers. There is a tendency to quickly call something revival because it reminds us of our preconceived notion. It also makes it harder to recognize any future revival that is different and fresh. The Promise Keepers movement is a very fine example of both dangers. Some immediately called it revival; others resist calling it revival because it is different.

One generation of the church has difficulty recognizing God at work in another generation. The contemporary church is largely composed of three distinct generations: the Builders, the Boomers, and the Busters.

It is common for a Builder to lament, saying, "Where have all the leaders gone? There are no new leaders." The reason for such a question is that Boomer or Buster leaders talk, dress, and think differently than Builder leaders. God is working in new ways through younger generations. The Builders know all the verses to "How Great Thou Art." Boomers know the first and last verses, but can sing along with the Eagles. Busters know the first phrase and think, *REM is now, my parents listen to the Eagles.*

The Builders all know Bev Shea, Cliff, the NAE, and missionary movements acronyms, such as MAF, SIM, OC, TEAM, and so on. Boomers have heard of some of that and the Four Spiritual Laws but are more interested in Leadership Network and the Saddlebacks, Wooddales, and Willow Creeks—the innovative islands of strength. Busters think Amy Grant is old; they respect what works and are focused on new ways to speak to their generation.

It is crucial that we don't allow our preconceived notions of what revival is to cause us to miss what God is doing right now. Let's just say that it won't involve a gospel quartet, a soloist's warbling, a large white tent with folding chairs, neon signs, or a loud suit. It could include a guy wearing a double-breasted suit with Nikes and a ponytail.

Do We Need Revival? 2

The need for revival is de facto. Very few would deny the cavernous gap between God's expectations and the church's reality. The church is always in need of renewal, some parts more than others. Some genres of the church are in serious decline, while others are on the rise. But one common denominator among both mainline and evangelical churches is an increasing shallowness and a selfishness powered by the engine of materialism. The church is not healthy, and its impact is hardly noticed by the general culture. What A. W. Tozer wrote shortly before his death still rings true. "A widespread revival of the kind of Christianity we know today in America might prove to be a moral tragedy from which we would not recover in a hundred years."[1] There has been little improvement.

The church is called to multiply, but if we export what we presently are, the results may be the vaccination of a generation with self-styled, self-willed, consumer faith that prevents the real disease—a truly transformed life. That is why revival, a widespread infusion of God's power and forgiveness, needs to precede any impact that will find its way into all the cleavages and crevices of American life. This does not mean the church is less responsible to diligently seek to live right and do right with what we've got right now. In God's good time he will sling us forward in his larger, ever-intentional redemptive rescue of humankind.

The church is always in need of renewal.

Health and Impact

A church's health and impact feed on and rely on each other. A sick church will talk about reproducing, but won't do it. But if the church waits for perfect health, it will never leave the safe confines of the sanctuary. Health and impact on society are simultaneous and interlocking.

Health

There is general agreement that the Western church is in a weakened state. George Barna reports in the International Religion Report that while 71 percent of the American public say there is no absolute truth, the fact that this view is shared by 40 percent of evangelical Christians is disappointing. In previous surveys Barna has found that more than 50 percent of Christians think that enjoying life and having a good time are the most important things in life.[2]

George Gallup has been giving Americans the Spiritual Fitness Assessment, and the findings are alarming. Gallup catalogs twelve characteristics to measure the power of Christ in people's lives. He found that:

- Only 13 percent of churchgoers are committed. This means they attend twice a month, serve in some capacity, and give financially to the church. This is down from 17 percent four years ago.
- 30 percent believe in reincarnation.
- 49 percent follow astrology.
- Four out of ten know who delivered the Sermon on the Mount.
- The churched are just as likely as the unchurched to participate in dishonest activity.[3]

Between Barna and Gallup there are volumes of statistics that confirm that the American church is in desperate need of spiritual depth. How would you like to engage the enemy with only 13 percent of your troops prepared to charge? What if they were very poorly educated in the faith and ill-prepared to carry out the mission or were not even aware there was a mission?

Church health explains to some degree if and when God sends revival, and when it does come, how long it lasts and what impact is made.

Revivals won't last, says John Schaar. "Evangelicals will have no lasting influence because the old lesson has not been learned. They still have no Christian mind. It is like an event in a cultural closet." Historian Martin Marty writes, "American Christians are more behaviors than believers. . . . we quietly slip into our comfortable subcultures and submit to its mores regardless if it can be supported by scripture." Church health explains to some degree if and when God sends revival, and when it does come, how long it lasts and what impact is made.

The training network I founded, T-NET International, has worked with more than five hundred churches. Each church receives a thousand days of consulting and coaching. This has revealed that only 19 percent of the members of these churches read the Bible and pray regularly (three times in seven days). That is up from 12 percent when the churches entered the transformational process. These are the crème de la crème: Instead of the pathetic 1.7 conversions per 100 adults attending the average church, the churches we work with have, right from the beginning, 8.0 conversions per 100 adults in worship. The fact that these churches operate at such a low level of fruitfulness should cause us to dial 911. We are not fit behaviorally or mentally. I know many say that we are educated beyond our behaviors, and that is true of some pockets of the church, but for the most part, Christians' ignorance of who God is and what he wants from us is massive.

Leadership

Most of the problems of health can be traced to one cause that lies behind most of the sickness cataloged above. The faithfulness and fruitfulness of a local church are determined by its leadership. Church consultant Win Arn surveyed one thousand churches, asking, "Why does the church exist?" He reported that 89 percent answered, "The church's purpose is to take care of my family's and my needs." Only 11 percent answered correctly, "The purpose of the church is to glorify God by making disciples and reaching the world for Christ."

When pastors were asked the same question, 90 percent got it right; only 10 percent said it was to take care of members.[4]

Barriers to Leadership

Connecting. How can there be such a difference between what pastors believe and the laity's opinion concerning the purpose of the church? The answer is not a rhetorical or dogmatic one; it is a communication issue. Pastors can say the right things but in a disconnected way. The laity often are required to piece together a philosophy of ministry concerning their church from the sermons. One week the pastor preaches on evangelism; the next week he powerfully communicates the power of loving relationships; the third week he champions helping the hungry and homeless; the fourth week it's world missions. Many pastors consider themselves visionary leaders and good communicators; they would be shocked to know how incoherent they sound to the congregation.

Teaching to obey. The second pastoral pathology is that pastors' structures are as archaic as their attempts to present systematic vision. A pastor's vision and the plans to accomplish the vision must match. Too often followers are uncertain how activity relates to goals, so they forget the vision and they lose enthusiasm for the activity. Teaching people to obey everything Christ commanded requires the vision of making disciples of all nations and a plan to start doing it right now in our church.

Modeling. This skill is the lost treasure of powerful communication in the church. The normal ethos of churches is to make leaders administrators, and people-to-people ministry is done by underlings, much like most businesses. The outcome then is a dearth of positive examples of what we are trying to accomplish.

Know-how. Where do pastors learn to lead? As Peter Drucker emphatically states after more than fifty years working with the world's greatest leaders, "There may be born leaders, but too few to depend on them. Leadership must be learned and can be learned." Drucker goes on to say, "The second major lesson is that 'leadership personality,' 'leadership style' and 'leadership traits' do not exist among the most effective leaders."[5]

So while the spiritual gift of leadership exists, it comes in various packages. There are far more pastors needed than people who have developed their spiritual gift of leadership. Therefore, it is imperative that we teach leadership and that pastors learn it. It is difficult to find a place in today's church where you can be taught to lead, how to present vision, and how to put into place structures that turn the vision into

39

reality. Most leaders must seek and find, learning by trial and error, because no one place provides all that is needed. A combination of local-church experience, seminary, training programs, seminars, good examples from fruitful churches, and patience and determination is required.

If the church doesn't change radically, God will continue to work, but not through institutional forms.

The first and most determinative cause of weakness and shallowness in churches lies at the feet of pastors. Most pastors are well intentioned and care deeply, but the training system is disconnected, scattered over the ecclesiastical world. As a result, leaders of congregations are not trained in systems nor in how to transform biblical imperatives into workable structures and plans. These issues will be carefully treated in the reformation section.

Impact

When leaders are not leading effectively, the penetration of the church on culture lacks sharpness. Instead of a cutting edge slicing into the layers of culture, the church impacts culture much like flying yogurt. There are reasons for such an anemic impact. The church has been marginalized. It has become like notes in the margins that surround the descriptions of what's happening in society.

The mission of the church is not to itself; its aim is to rescue humankind. As they take part, members get to participate and reap personal joy, purpose, and the care of a passionate God. But facts concerning the status of the church's mission are alarming. Not one county in the United States has experienced net church growth in the last ten years. This statistic includes mainline churches, which have seriously declined, and the liberal churches, which have lost their message.[6] But James Hunter's research also shocks many, since he reports that church attendance at evangelical churches has declined in the last thirty years.[7]

The four hundred fast-growing, successful megachurches in this country fog the real issues for 50 percent of the two hundred thousand congregations for whom the average attendance is fewer than seventy-five people. In spite of all the success and the championing of the Next Church (a term coined by Charles Trueheart in the *Atlantic Monthly*),[8] the ability of the church to reach the unchurched and bring about the conversions of seekers is in decline. The average church in America today sees 1.0 adult conversion per year, per one hundred in attendance. That means a church of two hundred would see 2.0 adult conversions. This might be expected of former mainline—now sidelined—churches but it is a surprise that evangelicals do only a tad better, 1.7 per one hundred in attendance.[9]

With respect to the ratio of numbers of people in church and the general population, the church is losing ground. The pie (the total national church attendance) isn't getting bigger. Only a few churches are excelling and they cannot compensate for the vast majority who are not.[10]

In *The Death of the Church*,[11] Mike Regele says that simply changing a few forms of the way we function is not good enough. If the church doesn't change radically, God will continue to work, but not through institutional forms. The metachurch, megachurch, and cell church are only tactical attempts to breathe new life into old structures. Churches are living on borrowed time, and many will not make it into the next century. What is needed is revolution, turning the church on its head. Get radical, like Jesus! Unless new leaders break new ground via iconoclastic attitudes, we will languish.

We are losing ground, the church is not keeping up with culture, with the population growth, or with the demands of the harvest. Fewer people are attending our churches, and it will get worse unless we commit ourselves to change.

Many good things are happening but not in sufficient quantity. It could also be argued that there is a lack of creative thinking and revolutionary activity getting at root causes and that the new leadership is simply too conservative. Old paradigms hold our minds hostage. We must look

41

for streams of daylight that have appeared through the cracks in our systems and run toward that daylight.

The way people are being occupied in the church world is connected to the pastor's leadership and to the hackneyed structures that dominate behaviors. These keep us from breaking out into great fruitfulness. We must find a way out.

Breakthroughs 3

A Recent History of God at Work

God is always in a revival mode. Again it is a matter of degree, not kind. Any person who seeks renewal can have it right now through true repentance and a behavioral change that matches the repentant decision (Luke 3:8; 2 Cor. 7:10; 1 John 1:9).

There is plenty of evidence that God has also made many attempts to bring his corporate church back to greatness. In the last twenty-five years evangelicals have succeeded in shooting onto contemporary culture's radar screen, only to have gradually lost altitude. They now are in danger of dropping off the screen. The Jesus movement gave energy to the launch that peaked in 1976 with *Time* magazine's declaration that it was "The Year of the Evangelical." That was quickly followed by the charismatic movement's ascendancy via the power of television.

Then came the church growth movement, an interesting mix of sociology, Scripture, and managerial technique. This created a network that increased the knowledge of models, methods, and techniques and then raised the pressure on pastors to succeed by a new, more contemporary standard. This was intensified by the endless parade of talented luminaries who had found the secret of success.

The eighties were punctuated by the megachurch and the metachurch, both of which proved irresistible to the American lust for success. The idea that such large numbers could be gathered so quickly shot adrenaline through pastoral veins.

The early nineties found the church under a siege of new realities that seriously threatened the eternal reality. With the recovery movement came a user-friendly twelve-step commitment that led to consumer Christians who take from a God who primarily gives and attend a church that caters to artificially stimulated needs.

Church consultants advise us, pollsters analyze us, psychologists counsel us, and pundits critique us. The evangelical bloodstream is clogged with dependency on professionalism and expertise. Its cardiovascular system has been weakened by a lack of the proper kind of exercise. The church has tried every kind of get-healthy method that violates God's simple laws of how to be a healthy Christian and how to have a fruitful church. We have strayed a great distance from Dietrich Bonhoeffer's description of the church: "The Church is the Church only when it exists for others."[1]

After twenty-five years of nifty ideas, talented luminaries, and new technologies that can put the Bible on CD-Rom and beam the world's best Bible teaching into any straw hut with direct TV, we've come up with very little impact. The good part is that evangelical leaders have never felt more needy, more repentant, and more hungry for God. Leaders who have integrity know when something isn't working.

The bad news is that evangelical church attendance as a percentage of population has decreased over the last twenty-five years. There has been a great deal of talk about exegeting our culture, reaching the unchurched, and user-friendly churches. Sadly, the facts demonstrate that while there is no shortage of talk, there is a dearth of effective outreach. Bearing fruit is the exception rather than the rule. We barely reach enough to replace those who have gone to heaven. The average church size in 1776 was 75.7; in 1890 it was 91.5 members. Today it is 100 members. Membership in churches and synagogues fell from 73 percent in 1937 to 65 percent in 1988. Church attendance has remained rather constant with respect to percentage of population, changing only from 41 percent in 1937 to 42 percent in 1988.[2]

> *If the conversion pie is not growing, then we are not advancing the kingdom as we should.*

The power of the new priesthood—namely, pundits, pollsters, consultants, and megachurch leaders—has been demonstrated in their ability to reverse the biblical flow. That flow has been and remains that the unbelieving world does not go to church, so the church must go to the unchurched world. But the magnetic appeal of these leaders attracts people to the church. Many leaders act as though they found a command in Scripture that non-Christians should go to church. I am not concerned here with the unusual pockets of power and fruitfulness that can be found in the church; those have been studied to death. My concern is the total gain by the total church. If the conversion pie is not growing, then we are not advancing the kingdom as we should.

Movements but No Breakthrough

A variety of movements have helped the cause but have not given the church the breakthrough that is expected and needed. Breakthrough is a measurable difference in three crucial areas:

1. The quality of spiritual character of the average church membership.
2. Some sign of penetration into culture with respect to large numbers of people coming to faith for the first time.
3. Some impact with respect to the level of general morality in popular culture as seen in films, television, and the allegiance to God in the public square.

At present the commitment level of Christians is in decline, as demonstrated by the Gallup Poll. Conversion rates are at an alarmingly low level, and culture continues to decay. All one needs do is listen to or watch one of the various daytime talk shows. They are demeaning; they divide people; they reflect the low ethical ebb of the entertainment industry. They value a dollar so much that they will both showcase and exploit the most pathetic of pathologies.

Great moral confusion in our culture exists concerning basic rights and wrongs. Generally people do not connect personal morality with public policy. Theological conviction is considered bigotry. One interesting observation is that some pundits accused Pat Robertson of being an anti-Semite for stating his orthodox viewpoint that even Jews outside of Christ will go to hell. At the same time they revered Mother Teresa, whose beliefs were even more narrow. The difference is public perception and the kind of work each was doing.

There is obvious confusion about theological position (Pat Robertson's beliefs) and behavior (how Robertson treats Jews). These are two very different things. Pat Robertson is fully committed to helping people; there is plenty of evidence of his compassion, if the press would look. But Americans have a difficult time thinking clearly about morality and religion, mainly because journalists are ignorant of these matters, and it all runs together to form critical mush.

Political Action

There have been aggressive efforts by Christians to bring righteousness to the earth. Such organizations as the Moral Majority and now the Christian Coalition have made and are making a qualitative difference. They have been able to move the larger moral issues to front and center. They have succeeded in getting certain people elected to public office, people who almost certainly would have had no real chance apart from the help of these groups.

While some good has been done, the long-term results are the marginalization and pollution of the church. Society has rightly or wrongly determined that the church should stay out of politics and intentionally reacted to the frontal assault by moving the church to the side.

The pollution of the church is seen in its arrogance and ignorance. The arrogance has been witnessed in unseemly displays of hubris when a battle was won. In the words of Vince Lombardi, who scolded his players for spiking the football after a touchdown, "When you get into the end zone, act like you've been there before." Christians should accept victory with grace and humility.

The church's ignorance is observed in its inability to understand what really makes a moral difference. True moral difference is a heart issue. In a democracy you cannot enforce a law that a society will not support.

Church Growth Movement

Even Peter Wagner questioned the effectiveness of the voluminous charts, graphs, and techniques produced by the movement he helped start. He simply stated concerning church growth principles, "Somehow they don't work."[3] Church growth principles in a supporting role to prayer, a theology of mission, and high-commitment Christian community can enhance any church. But when the prerequisites are missing, too often church growth spawns superficial churches pastored by insecure programmatic junkies. Then overall attendance stagnates, and Christians are trained to think like consumers. God becomes the ultimate in "room service."

The Charismatic Movement

A good friend and charismatic theologian told me, "After thirty years of 'name it and claim it,' 'let go and let God,' and the 'healthy wealthy' heresy, the goose bumps are gone and we have no theology." While the charismatic movement has helped other evangelicals release God from the theological prisons we have built for him, there have also been the silly and embarrassing escapades that have discredited us and subsequently have been burned into the national psyche. Television has largely proven to be a curse for the church with respect to effectively reaching Americans. This is why the late Malcolm Muggeridge claimed that if the incarnation had taken place in our contemporary framework, Satan would have added a fourth wilderness temptation, the offer of a nationally syndicated television program.

I find it a positive development that the charismatic revival has now been successfully assimilated into mainstream evangelical life. In the end, however, even the energy of this movement has not advanced the kingdom in a satisfactory fashion.

Prophetic Schematics

Prophetic literature has been instrumental in bringing many to Christ and in stimulating others to study the Bible in great detail. There is tremendous interest on the part of the general and Christian public in how the world will end and who wins. I am afraid, however, that in recent years it has become much ado about very little.

Too many evangelicals have adopted entire theological end-times packages without study. The evangelical subculture is very powerful and sometimes forces an entire genre of Christian faith on its people. For example the dispensation package includes at least a "curtsy" to *The Late Great Planet Earth* and the pretribulation rapture.

> *Television has largely proven to be a curse for the church with respect to effectively reaching Americans.*

There is so much disagreement about the details of the end times that most leaders no longer think about it. Most leaders who are committed to national revival and the fulfillment of the Great Commission have forgotten the details and don't think it important enough to revisit their views. That is why so many once-grand prophecy conferences are dead or on life support. In the context of today's priorities the battle cry is "Jesus is coming back, and I want to be ready."

Again the prophetic movement has not helped the church penetrate unchurched networks sufficiently to have improved the numbers of conversions.

The Parachurch Movement

The surge of ministries alongside the local church has been very helpful. A strong case could be made that God raised up the parachurch to save the institutional church from oblivion. By their very nature parachurch works have served to perform important corrective measures for the church and are largely responsible for training and providing today's evangelical leadership. Any objective churchman would be compelled to fall to his knees and thank God for the powerful contribution of parachurch ministries to the local church. But movements tend to take on a life of their own and have taken on certain roles that the church should be performing. Major movements such as Campus Crusade for Christ, the Navigators, and the Billy Graham Evangelistic Association provide leadership for the church.

In the end, however, the fact must be faced that the church is still rather anemic. One only wonders what it would be like *without* the parachurch. Thank God for the Billy Grahams and Bill Brights of this age.

The issue is the health of the church itself: What is happening every day in the local church? What is the pastor doing or thinking he is doing? What are the church leaders doing, and how do they understand their roles and the purpose of their congregations? Only at that level will the difference be made and the church break through.

Three New and Encouraging Movements

The Prayer Movement

Recently I was privileged to attend a prayer and fasting gathering called by Dr. Bill Bright. It made a great impact on my life, as it did on hundreds of other Christian leaders in attendance. The prayer movement now has thousands attending prayer gatherings. Thousands of leaders from virtually every genre of Christianity are able to agree together in prayer for two things: that God will pour out his Spirit on America and that the Great Commission will be fulfilled in our lifetime.

A strong case could be made that God raised up the parachurch to save the institutional church from oblivion.

I don't believe the church will break out to effective change without a great deal of corporate prayer and fasting. But even with the energy that revival would bring, it must be joined to other factors. I deal with these in the reformation section.

Promise Keepers

Former Colorado football coach Bill McCartney has led this effort to help men restore integrity to their families, their work, and their churches. This movement has all the markings of a work blessed and energized by God. Its growth and its acceptance by the church are two such markings. But when the meetings end, the real challenge begins. The men must return to their homes, jobs, and churches. Will the support structure be in place? Will there be leadership (particularly pastoral leadership) to capture and channel the energy of the inspired men? The action must be in the church. This is where the final validation takes place.

Great Commission Networks

A new crop of cooperative networks have emerged from the great concern for the reaching of our world and cities. Birthed in the 1974 and 1990 Lausanne conferences in Lausanne, Switzerland, and Manila of the Philippines has come A.D. 2000 and Beyond. The U.S. expression is Mission America, chaired by Dr. Paul Cedar.

The denominational walls are coming down, egos are being deflated, and God is pleased by the combined efforts to evangelize the world. The beauty of this is that people of every evangelical ilk are praying together, working together, and agreeing before God together to reach our land. We should be encouraged, but not misled. The larger gatherings can and, I believe, will bring revival to our country and unity to the body. But equal in importance to what begins renewal movements is what stops them, what impedes them, what wastes them, and finally what sustains them.

A Jump-Start

Each movement considered has fired its best shot to help the church: political action aimed at society, the church growth movement aimed at numerical growth and relevancy, the charismatics aimed at worship and power, the parachurch aimed at neglected mission, the Promise Keepers aimed at the home, and Great Commission Networks aimed at cooperative world evangelization. All these efforts are

51

Having leaders who know how to lead a church in intentional disciple making is the single greatest need of the church today.

God's way of attempting to jump-start his church. Each serves as an encouragement and a reminder, an encouragement that the mission can be done and a reminder that every local church is to reach its own community.

If these movements do not channel their energy through the local churches, that energy will have a shorter "shelf life." The church can harness and channel the power of new ideas and motivated people. The church touches people at the level where life is actually lived, where they work and play. All other expressions of mission are secondary and supportive of local churches. But churches must be ready. They must understand their mission and know how to handle excited men returning from a Promise Keepers gathering.

Churches must join hands with various energetic movements for both to succeed. Pastors and church leaders cannot learn these things in weekend seminars or video workshops. They must receive ongoing, hands-on help. Having leaders who know how to lead a church in intentional disciple making is the single greatest need of the church today. Disciple making is greatly misunderstood, for all the talk about it. Leaders often know little about how to train people in the context of their church. The irony is, of course, that there is no environment better suited for discipleship than the church.

Barriers 4

With attendance down, selfishness up, and conversion growth slowed to the speed of only replacing the dead, no one would propose that the church has broken through to a new era of fruitfulness. What barriers keep stopping us at the very door of revival and reformation?

It is not the failure to go after and mimic the successful megachurches. Studying success is always interesting but in the long run doesn't lead to change; it leads to discouragement. Even if 40 percent of evangelical church attendees do go to the four hundred churches of two thousand or more in attendance, it does no good for the other 60 percent to try to become something they're not. It doesn't work! More important, becoming like someone other than Jesus has very little to do with God's will for the church. Why dedicate yourself to what can't be reproduced? There is great value in adopting principles and attitudes of fruitful churches, but most fruitful churches do not have two thousand or more congregants; just the famous ones do. The unwritten law of becoming a megachurch is: The leader must be a captivating personality with wide public appeal that is congruent to his time and culture. Frankly, that is less than 1 percent of the general population.

Major Disconnect

Our pursuit of God is incomplete. We are good at holding meetings and talking about and praying for renewal but we remain unprepared. The prophet Isaiah spoke for God and gave us the answer. God commanded Isaiah to speak to his people about their rebellion. His full-throated cry, at the top of his voice, sounds out over our land today. "For day after day they seek me out; they seem eager to know my ways, as if they were a nation that does what is right and has not forsaken the commands of its God. They ask me for just decisions and seem eager for God to come near them" (Isa. 58:2).

This stinging indictment proves man's basic nature hasn't changed in nearly twenty-seven hundred years. The people are doing the right things with respect to words; they seem to be interested, says God. I think it could be said that the Western church seems to be interested in seeking God. We hold many meetings to discuss, pray, and figure out how we can break through to a higher level of spiritual health and fruitfulness. But like our spiritual predecessors, our thirst remains unquenched.

"Why have we fasted, they say, and you have not seen it? Why have we humbled ourselves, and you have not noticed?" (Isa. 58:3a). We say, "Hey, God! We have held solemn assemblies, thousands of leaders have prayed and fasted for three days, pastors are meeting, we see great unity in seeking your blessing. Haven't you noticed? Are you going to act? What must we do? Isn't this what you want?" The people are confused because they thought all that was necessary was to worship God with all they had and really mean it. The people's sincerity is not in question, but their conduct is. The duplicity between word and deed make their sincere efforts of worship insulting to God.

God answers in Isaiah 58:3b–5a: "Yet on the day of your fasting, you do as you please and exploit all your workers. Your fasting ends in quarreling and strife. . . . You cannot fast as you do today and expect your voice to be heard on high." God actually scoffs at their great symbolic display that lacks integrity. "Is this the kind of fast I have chosen, only a day for a man to humble himself?"

The major disconnect in the Western church is our resistance to changing our cultural ways that cause society to doubt our sincerity.

I don't want a day, I want your life! God is saying. He goes on to explain: "Is not this the kind of fasting I have chosen: to loose the chains of injustice and untie the cords of the yoke, to set the oppressed free and break every yoke? Is it not to share your food with the hungry and to provide the poor wanderer with shelter—when you see the naked, to clothe him, and not to turn away from your own flesh and blood?" (Isa. 58:6–7).

This reminds us of Samuel's words to a disobedient Saul, "To obey is better than sacrifice, and to heed is better than the fat of rams" (1 Sam. 15:22).

Christians still resist the penetrating truth that obedience and integrity of life are connected to God's answering prayer in the affirmative. The major disconnect in the Western church is our resistance to changing our cultural ways that cause society to doubt our sincerity.

The research cited earlier by both Gallup and Barna reveals a materialistic church, dominated and tamed by its culture. We have largely lost our edge and our ability to penetrate our land. God doesn't respect a church that holds a lot of meetings, then goes home and behaves the same as before. God's Word is plain enough. He tells us to start caring for each other and those around us. If our message and mission match, then God will bless us. "Then you will call and the LORD will answer; you will cry for help, and he will say: Here am I" (Isa. 58:9).

What sweet words! "Here am I." God yearns to meet us, to revive us, to saturate us in his love, forgiveness, and power. But we must understand that part of the formula is to repent and turn away from both personal and corporate sin. Attitudes need to change, but so do our actions. Those actions are not only personal lifestyle choices but corporate choices by the church as to how we organize and what we spend our money on. We need to demonstrate an integrity to God and the world that we are ready to spread his blessing.

The classic concept of chasing rabbit trails is that you are hunting bigger game, but you keep forgetting your objective and settle for much less. God is not going to punish a pastor or other leader for not being a captivating personality. He very well may discipline a leader for trying to become one. It is pathetic to watch people impersonate others. It is bad enough to imitate Elvis, George Burns, or other departed personalities. But it is heartbreaking to watch church leaders, especially pastors, try to be who they are not and live up to a standard, not set by God but set by a media-market culture. At least Elvis impersonators have a real life; sadly these pastors have no other life.

> *God is not going to punish a pastor or other leader for not being a captivating personality. He very well may discipline a leader for trying to become one.*

It is so liberating to be the person God made you to be and to settle for the best you can do. It is just as refreshing for the pundits and especially the congregation to say in response, "Yes, this is good; this is God's will; yes, this is the point."

One of the great moments of my life was when I realized I did not have the wide personality appeal of some people I admired. I found that when that dream died, I could get on with my life. I know very few leaders who have been placed on a high pedestal who actually pursued it. Those who have pursued it usually don't last.

None of us like to consider ourselves average, but someone needs to fill that role! The good news is that the average person who walks faithfully with God and perseveres will be anything but average. The "big game" we all pursue is being both faithful and fruitful in our walk with and work for God. But the "rabbit trails" we often end up pursuing are fame, notice of our friends and colleagues, or seeking to build a big church. There is nothing wrong with a megachurch—I wish I had one—but that is not God's plan for me and for most of you. So I thank God for his marvelous expressions of power and grace in megachurches. Then I "get a life," "get over it," and "get on with it." I won't settle for less than the best: God working through me as only he can. I hope you have come to this point in your life as well. Learn all you can, work hard, strive for excellence, then just thank God that he lets you do this stuff!

There are three specific barriers that act as a commentary on the above disconnect found in Isaiah—the disconnect between words and deeds. These three barriers form a large wall that the church has been hitting its head against for at least a half century.

Barrier One: The domestication of the church, because it has marginalized the individual's impact by a subcultural definition of what it means to be "spiritual." *This relates primarily to the individual.*

Barrier Two: The Christendom paradigm, because it keeps the local church from reorganizing for effectiveness. *This relates primarily to the local church.*

Barrier Three: Denominations, because they are systemically blocking renewal rather than empowering it. *This relates primarily to national expressions of the church.*

A word about systemic issues: All three barriers are about systemic problems at the personal, local, and national levels. This is not a reflection on people. We are primarily passive recipients of our culture and our systems. We are good people trapped in bad systems.

These barriers must come down!

Domestication of the Church

Barrier One: *The domestication of the church has marginalized the individual's impact by a subcultural definition of what it means to be "spiritual."* The church is "housebroken"; its ability to penetrate culture, to reap a great harvest, has been compromised. There are places the church isn't allowed to go and institutions we are not allowed to officially influence. The liberal church has been marginalized by the same leftist political agenda that has robbed mainline churches of their message. The evangelical church has narrowed its impact through its rationalization and packaging of spirituality. Add to this the mistaken mission, in recent years, of ushering in a new era of morality via political activists. For many the line between scripturally driven conviction and one's party platform has disappeared. Culture thoroughly dominates much of the U.S. church world. So many Christians, left and right, simply repeat their religious or political mantras. But culture's hold on the church is no tighter than on the evangelical's understanding of spirituality and what really counts.

Accommodation to Culture

Culture's hold on the church was slammed home to me on one of my trips to Europe. A godly young German pastor was carefully driving me on the autobahn at one hundred miles per hour to my speaking assignment. Eventually we had to exit the highway to reach the small island where the conference was to be held. We passed through a number of small towns. Every city looked much the same, neat and quaint. Towering above everything else was the town brewery.

As an American evangelical whose mind is always occupied with moral trivia, I asked, "Do German pastors drink beer?"

"Of course," the pastor replied. "A pastor who does not drink beer would be an outsider, not one of us."

I let that soak in for a few miles. "Will they be serving beer at the pastor's conference?" I asked.

"No." He laughed. "But we will fill up the beer gardens after you speak."

The idea of four hundred pastors rushing out to get a beer is a thought that contorts the mind of an American evangelical. In one of the question and answer sessions I was asked what I thought of German pastors. I responded, "I am thinking of becoming one. I can drive as fast as I want and drink all the beer I want!" They laughed twice, some at the English version, others at the translation.

Isn't it odd that I can be a godly pastor in Germany, drive one hundred miles per hour, drink a couple of beers a day, and be highly revered? I hop a 747 to New York, get off the plane, engage in the same behavior and I am regarded a sinner by colleagues and I get fired by my church for knocking down a brew. I have always found it frustrating that the Christian subculture defines right and wrong as powerfully as Scripture, and often traditional opinion overrules the Bible.

I am not asking readers to change their personal convictions on the gray areas; I am asking you to think! How much of what we believe and practice, commend or condemn others for is really biblically based? The sluggish and myopic thinking of leaders has created a church that largely cannot respond to the needs around us because we are trapped in our little burrows of parochialism. The fact that many who read this will only remember that I didn't hammer drinking proves my point. They won't get the point, because it is like pointing out something to my dog, who only sniffs my finger. He does not understand that I am pointing at something else. Some of the accommodations are much more serious than a glass of beer. Unless we can get over the minutiae of moralism, we

The church is "housebroken"; its ability to penetrate culture, to reap a great harvest, has been compromised.

won't be able to respond. We will not be ready for God to send revival, and God's effort would be largely wasted.

Rationalization of Spirituality

I am among a body of writers who have warned the church against materialism, secularism, and various narcissistic behaviors. Many of us believe the greatest single engine in the destruction of the Protestant ethic was the invention of instant credit. No longer does anyone need to work and save, delay gratification, or avoid gluttonous self-indulgence. There are very few people left like my grandfather, B. G. Butler. He saved his money, and every ten years, when he went out and got himself a brand new Chevy, he paid cash!

Many of us believe the greatest single engine in the destruction of the Protestant ethic was the invention of instant credit.

Neal Postman's critique of a nation, *Amusing Ourselves to Death,* demonstrates that television feeds our lust and lowers the level of discourse to demagoguery, which leads to the "dumbing down" of a nation.[1] These powerful cultural forces are eating away at the national character. But very little has been written about how culture has limited the power and spirituality of the church—at least in the direction that I now go at my own peril.

In the 1940s evangelicalism emerged with the founding of several new organizations that were to give conservatives more cultural acceptance and to prove they didn't have a "tin ear" for culture. At the same time evangelicals began a process that led to the methodization and standardization of spirituality.

This was not an intentional process; it simply reflected existing culture and a cognitive systems approach to other parts of life. Naturally practitioners would try to make spirituality more understandable, give it some measurable handles.

60

James Hunter explains, "The spiritual aspects of Evangelical life . . . [are] principles, rules, steps, laws, codes, guidelines, and such. The proliferation in the Evangelical book market of how-to manuals for channeling the many dimensions of Christian life is evidence of this tendency."[2]

This packaging and measuring of spirituality based on rules and steps has led to faulty images of what is spiritual and has influenced people's behavior. From the outset the newcomer to the wonderful world of church lives in a highly systematized environment that is heavy with formula. After a short period of time in church, the newcomer learns that being spiritual means measuring up to the expectations. Attempting to sort out what God expects from what my version of Christianity expects becomes challenging. I became a Christian in connection with a certain version of church. I learned quickly that certain behaviors were considered very spiritual. If I raised my hands in worship and said amen at the right times, I would be considered really "with it."

> *This packaging and measuring of spirituality based on rules and steps has led to faulty images of what is spiritual and has influenced people's behavior.*

If I could testify that God had spoken to me or that I cried during my prayer time and that God was giving me a new freedom in my "prayer language," this was a sign that I was mature. Certain spiritual gifts were more highly esteemed than others. The people with the gifts of helps and mercy could serve refreshments and run errands for those who exercised the gifts of healings or prophecy. In this environment, being slain in the Spirit was as predictable as the offering. This genre of the church had its ethos, its rewards, and its punishments like every other. It really is not better or worse than any other version; it does, however, narrow the options. The growth of the church was much more like cloning than multiplication.

The misunderstanding of these activities can be the greatest barrier of all to spiritual awakening. It also demonstrates the degree to which the church has accommodated itself to culture. People have come to confuse activity with significant amounts of time in activities as a means of being more spiritual and pleasing to God. Being spiritual has become the endgame of following Jesus. I would like to explore one example of misunderstanding what is spiritual: the packaging of devotional life.

The Devotional Life

Does the Bible really say that you need to spend at least thirty minutes in prayer every day or you cannot be intimate with God? Does it say that the longer you pray, the more power you have? Does God measure power by our knowledge of Bible content? Is it really true that if you miss your "quiet time," after one day you know it, after two days your family knows it, and after three days everyone knows it? Are people who pray two hours a day closer to God than those who pray fifteen minutes a day? Do amounts of time in prayer have any direct relationship to obedience and fruitfulness? My answer to all the above is NO!

I had been a Christian a few months when I received a note in my dorm mailbox. It invited me to a meeting on Saturday morning at 7:00 A.M. This is a nonstarter for most college students. What a ridiculous idea!

I went. I discovered that a professor had chosen two people to mentor, and I was one of them. He proposed that over the next nine months we learn to study the Bible by working through Romans and memorizing seventy Scripture verses. So we embarked on the journey, and it proved to be seminal. It set my course and taught me the value of spending time with God. It also set in my mind a damaging falsehood—that I needed a daily "quiet time," or my walk with God would be desperately weak.

After learning this falsehood, I often thought I was really out of fellowship with God because I had missed my prayers or found watching sports a lot more interesting. I expected that as I grew I would spend more and more hours in prayer and Bible study, because it would be second nature, natural, and would get easier with time. This expectation led me to a great deal of guilt and wasted time. As I have grown spiritually over the last twenty-eight years, some things have cleared up for me.

I write this with fear and trembling because the evangelical subculture still has a very firm grip on my mind. But I plunge on because today I walk intimately with God based on what the Bible actually teaches, not on other people's expectations.

I learned that I needed to interact with God on a regular basis. That might mean thirty minutes one day, then no formal time for three days, then ninety minutes of concentrated time. The principle was to combine obeying God with talking with God. There are many people who do the "quiet time" thing very faithfully, but there is no impact on their life. It is simply an empty ritual. The way I interact with God is a combination of temperament, schedule, profession, and spiritual wiring. We are charged with the responsibility to develop ways to interact with God's Word and with God himself via prayer. But to set a sixteenth-century Catholic monk's practice as the standard for time in prayer for a busy attorney is to confuse the issue. The principle is that we need to regularly talk to God. Does God hear us when we are on our knees at 5:30 A.M. better than at 11:30 while we drive to a luncheon? Is it more spiritual or powerful to beg God for something for one hour or simply to believe him when we ask the first time? What impresses us is not very important to God. He is concerned about our hearts, our attitudes, our faith.

I don't intend to discourage those like myself who prefer a more structured approach to interacting with God. I still start my day reading Scripture and praying. That is comfortable for me as a religious professional.

We are told, in contrast to public displays of prayer, we are to enter our private prayer place (Matt. 6:6). Two common abuses to this exhortation exist. First, there are those who say Jesus was telling us not to pray in public, so praying before meals in restaurants, before sporting events, or at graduations

Today the thirty-minute quiet time is virtually impossible for many. There is very little margin left in the high-demand, high-stress environment.

is "showy"; prayer is a private matter. The other abuse is to insist that we have one physical location that we go to every day and spend a certain time there praying until God speaks. For the present-day saint a prayer closet is thirty minutes in traffic—turn off the radio, the cellular phone, and be alone with God. Walking with God is to pray continuously, to practice the presence of God. This fast-moving disciple keeps his prayer journal on the sun visor.

Some people's gifts and life circumstances allow them to be "prayer warriors," to spend extended times in prayer. There are examples in the Bible of Jesus praying all night, of fasting and praying for forty days, of being in serious agonizing prayer, such as the Gethsemane experience. I believe there are times for special prayer, for extended prayer, for prayer and fasting. There are times when life's circumstances warrant long times in prayer. Both Testaments indicate that perseverance in prayer has its place as well as simply "pray and believe" (Mark 11:24; Luke 11:1–10). I have done all of the above and treasure those prayer times but I don't confuse them with the modern invention called "quiet time."

Today the thirty-minute quiet time is virtually impossible for many. There is very little margin left in the high-demand, high-stress environment. Many of the classic approaches to the spiritual life were developed in the seventeenth and eighteenth centuries. It is crucial that they be seen for what they are—man-made methods to act out a principle. That is fine; we must do this in every age. They reflected the period of their origin. "They often require a degree of leisure and absence of personal pressure that are totally unrealistic in the midst of the stresses and tensions of modern Western Life. Whatever their past greatness, they have often proved unworkable in the modern era."[3]

Alister McGrath goes on to speak of what respected leaders advocated in the past:

Many leaders counseled new Christians to read their Bibles daily; without this daily spiritual nourishment, they could expect to starve and lose their spiritual vitality. This advice, given forty years ago, has become increasingly problematic with the changes in the pace of living . . . their faith comes to be made dependent on something that cannot be sustained in the long term.[4]

Thus the practice of the spiritual disciplines becomes an end in itself, rather than a means to the end of knowing and walking with God.

Revival and Packaged Formulas

Do we really want to multiply and export the highly formalized version of evangelical subcultural life through revival? For the church to break through we must throw out our bent to clone. There are clear biblical rights and wrongs, but we erroneously still give "bonus" points for heroic efforts to conform to moralistic norms. It would really be sad if revival only managed to get Christians and new converts to stop dancing and going to questionable films. It would be meaningless if revival meant every Christian added ten minutes to his or her quiet time. This "revival" would not impact our mission, and the devil wouldn't care. We have inadvertently walled ourselves in with our evangelical subculture. Explosives will be required for us to get out. Then we can have an impact.

A New-Paradigm Person

It's not just what Christians stop; it is what they start! The stops and starts need some fresh air. If we stop gossiping, then we start encouraging; if we stop hating, we start doing loving things for our enemies. We stop cheating on our spouse and start nourishing him or her; we stop our lavish lifestyle and start giving generously to those in need. We stop being critical of the church and start creative ministries. Real change is discarding what is old and replacing it with something new. That takes time, the creativity of the Holy Spirit, and the help of the church.

Spirituality is measured not only by engagement in certain activities, such as the proper perspective and use of the spiritual disciplines.[5] Spirituality means the church gives guidance in the beginning to new Christians, but allows them to grow and find their own way of relating to God based on spiritual giftedness, temperament, and God's missional calling. It means that the community of Christ does not ostracize the daring and the new expressions of outreach that don't include sawdust and "Just As I Am."

An exuberant new Christian in our church wanted to take young people rock climbing. The elders told him that this was risky, that the church had no insurance, and that they knew of no other church that did anything like this. And what about kids who don't climb? He did it anyway, by convincing parents to come along and "hold the rope." Parents didn't have to climb, but their presence took care of the insurance liability. The next year he led eighty rock climbers to Christ; many of them were parents, who were the rope holders.

The church is packed with passionate people who can reach others if we allow it.

The new-paradigm Christian is founded in character. The development of this character allows our minister of rock climbing to care enough to create that kind of ministry. This Christian character, found in a variety of passages, is succinctly described in John 15:7–13.

1. A disciple interacts with Christ via the Word and prayer (15:7).
2. A disciple has a powerful impact (15:8).
3. A disciple displays an integrity of life (15:9–10).
4. A disciple has personal contentment (15:11).
5. A disciple loves others sacrificially (15:12–13).

This foundation of Christian character makes possible a lifetime of walking in the Spirit. Once the foundation is laid, the spiritual giftedness and creativity emerge that God uses to penetrate the world for Christ. Yes, the church will need to train, care for, and guide the person. But take off the harness, shut down the cloner, and allow God to express himself uniquely through each disciple and the church.

Marginalization in the Church

James Hunter writes, "The amount of time a person spends reading the Bible, praying, tithing, witnessing, and orienting his life goals around God's will all provide empirical indexes by which the differences between the carnal Christian and the spiritual Christian are elucidated in the Evangelical world view."[6] I would fully encourage all Christians to engage in the above activities. My point of contention is the phrase, "The amount of time a person spends." This means we have left out the nonreader, noncontemplative, nonverbal person with a different set of gifts and ways of expression than the average church member. Can one interact with God's Word as a nonreader? Yes, millions do it via the spoken word, stories, and the preached word on video, audiotape, and the radio. Much of the world is still in this posture.

Much of the church is marginalized because members of the body don't fit into the predetermined package and formula for spirituality. Those who do fit into the package close themselves off from the outside world. At the same time the church has softened its message. Many Christians don't want to appear intolerant by saying that Christ is the only way of salvation and hell is a reality for the nonbeliever. It is almost impossible to get an evangelical to directly answer the question, "Are those who don't commit to Christ going to hell?" Most orthodox Christians want to say yes, but so few of us do. We are labeled bigots and fascists; then it gets really bad!

Scripture tells us to be wise in our conduct: "Be wise in the way you act toward outsiders; make the most of every opportunity. Let your conversation be always full of grace, seasoned with salt, so that you may know how to answer everyone" (Col. 4:5–6). That means we must use terms and explain the truth of Christ in ways that don't needlessly alienate. But to be sure, to tell the truth in this culture is scandalous!

A demeanor change is good; an editing of the message is not. I have seen too many leaders "fold in the clutch" on national television when confronted by the press with issues of exclusive versus inclusive theological questions. (I have folded myself several times by avoiding the direct answer.) I don't want to demean people I respect, but when confronted with the big question—Will unbelievers go to hell?—they have skirted it and have not answered in the way we know they believe.

> *Domestication means we have lost our impact inside the church culture because of a decline in the integrity of the biblical standards of living.*

Domestication means we have lost our impact inside the church culture because of a decline in the integrity of the biblical standards of living. We have also lost our impact outside in general culture. This barrier to our impact on both the church and the world must be dealt with as we prepare for a special visit from God.

The Ineffective Church

Barrier Two: *The Christendom paradigm has kept the local church from reorganizing for effectiveness.* The comfortable and satisfied say, "If it ain't broke, don't fix it." Change agents respond, "If it ain't broke, break it." Neither extreme applies to the contemporary church. The church is broken; we just don't want to admit it. The church's failure to make real gains in the harvest and its inability to penetrate culture and effect moral change are reasons enough to consider it "broke."

At present we are sending little light out into the darkness, and our saltiness has lost its ability to preserve the morality levels of life. Church history is littered with examples of people unwilling to face the reality of decline. To live in decline is to let the church break down.

Church consultant Bob Gilliam points out three kinds of church paradigms that are common and broken. In fact these represent most churches presently in operation in the Western hemisphere.

1. The Institutionalized Church

The focus of the institutionalized church is preaching and maintenance. There is no real leadership development. The same people just rotate to new positions by nomination. The power is in the hands of the church board, certain committees, and each person's length of service. Help for spiritual growth comes mainly through the Sunday school and fellowship groups. The root values of the institutionalized church are traditional, according to the relational caste system, where power is localized in a certain group of people and kept from others.

> *The church is broken; we just don't want to admit it.*

2. The Voluntary Association Church

In the voluntary association church singing in the choir is equal to prayer and reaching the unchurched is no more vital than Christian socials where people can share their lives. This is a church void of priorities; everything is equal. It is a totally tolerant environment that has the impact of a blob of Jell-O. This church is built on the foundation of American democracy. Democracy is fine in the general, pluralistic culture, but when practiced in the church, it reduces leadership to counting votes. The pastor is almost forced to act like the "party whip" in Congress, who garners and counts the votes. In this church, everyone's opinion is equal. No distinction is made between the spiritual person's thoughts and the carnal Christian with a "chip" on one shoulder. The church becomes an amalgamation of interest groups where every voice must be heard and every faction should be represented on the board.

What a mess!

3. The Unintentional Church

In the unintentional church, leaders and followers cannot describe the kind of person they are trying to produce. There is no "this is our business" certainty; therefore, when everything is the church, nothing is the church. There is no sequential process that is widely known by which persons could be hopeful that they were going to make spiritual progress in that church. There is no plan to develop people in any systematic way. There is also no system in place to develop people in such a way that a new Christian could become a leader by design. It would all need to just sort of happen.

Paradigms Lost

The real barrier to an effective church, according to Loren Mead in *The Once and Future Church,* is the loss of the *Apostolic paradigm* and its replacement with the *Christendom paradigm.*[7] Paradigms are about patterns of behavior and the rules and regulations we use to construct those patterns. We use those patterns first to establish boundaries and then to direct us on how to solve problems. The church has difficulty breaking out and breaking through because leaders underappreciate the power of cultural paradigms.

I was a thirty-four-year-old Californian when I arrived in a provincial midwestern city to pastor a rigid church that was strongly locked into the Christendom paradigm. One of the expectations found in the pastoral pantheon was "If you go into the hospital, the pastor visits you." I did visit people in their hour of need, and I did it gladly.

The pastor who preceded me, however, set an unrealistic standard. He worked eighty hours a week. He was a "human love machine"; not only was he a caring person, he had the enviable quality of being able to make people feel loved. If you went into the hospital, this pastor would beat you there! I loved the people; I just had a hard time convincing them that I did. An elderly woman went to the hospital for care, and for some reason still unidentified, I missed it. I didn't go. She started a not-so-holy crusade via the telephone: "That pastor is no man of God. There I was in the hospital, and he never came." This is when I learned if you somehow mistreat a person who in the minds of the church is helpless, you're toast!

This matter was serious enough that I called on her in her home. "Well, Mrs. Offended Christian," I cheerfully stated, "I understand you were upset that you were not visited in the hospital?"

"Yes," she sniped.

Being a novice at such discussions, I formed a penetrating question, "Could you tell me why that bothers you?"

"Well, Pastor." She pursed her lips. "I'm surprised you need to ask that."

"No, really." I leaned forward. "I really want to know why having the pastor visit you is so vital. In fact," I went on, "I know that more than ten people came to see you. They were not paid. They had to come during visiting hours. They had no special clergy parking permit. Did you appreciate them?"

"Of course." Now she was huffing. "Pastors have always done this; that is what they do."

"Yes, I know," I answered, "but could you tell me why? Could you cite a biblical reference for the pastor needing to do it rather than others in the congregation?"

"Young man," she bristled, "you are the theologian, you know the answer." This was proof that she had never met a real theologian.

I thought it was time I made my point. "Ma'am." I leaned forward. "You are familiar with the Scripture in First Corinthians chapter twelve concerning the different parts of the body of Christ and the fact they are equal in value but have different functions?"

"Oh, yes," she responded. "I don't like all that weird stuff, all that tongues-talking stuff, but the rest is fine."

"You know it says that the hand should not say to the foot, because you are not a hand, you are a less important part of the body. You remember that, don't you?" I was closing in.

71

"Of course," she snapped.

"I think what has happened here is that you wanted to be visited by a hand. Instead, you were visited by three kneecaps and four toes. And what concerns me is how you have elevated my importance far too much and have devalued the gracious ministry of others."

I made a very powerful and biblically sound argument, and she didn't buy it. In fact she got worse and, until her day of departure into heaven, was convinced I was wrong and someday would see the light. This is a quaint example of the Christendom paradigm on which logic and biblical presentation have little effect. Because it is a worldview, a way of thinking, it doesn't have a slot for the idea that pastoral care is a ministry given to the entire body, not just the clergy. God has gifted many who are not clergy to be involved and even lead a church's caring ministry.

When we endeavor to change, we must break the paradigm and then start over from zero. Therefore, we need to understand the principles.[8] Those principles are scriptural and will be examined in the reformation section. For now, however, I want to look at Mead's treatment of the two primary church paradigms.

The Apostolic Paradigm

The apostolic model of the church was and is based on two concepts: *apostellein,* the Greek word "to send," and *ekklesia,* "the called out," translated *church.* The church was then an army of people called out from the world and sent by God on a mission to rescue the world (2 Cor. 5:18–21). Beyond the front door of the church was a frontier to be conquered. The world was not neutral. Christians were aliens operating in a hostile environment, offering the world what it desperately needed and powerfully resisted. This understanding of the church grew and flourished through the first century but began to decline in the late second and early third century. It began to die under Emperor Constantine, when the church became legal in A.D. 313. It is this model to which the church needs to return.

The Christendom Paradigm

This paradigm began with Emperor Constantine in A.D. 313, when the church became legal and accepted. It took several centuries to fully develop and is now faithfully practiced by the Builder generation in a local church near you. The classic Christendom model had common characteristics.

And the two shall become one. When the royals run the church, pay the clergy, and determine their mission, all hostility between a secular society and the "called-out ones" disappears. The church and state become identical; to be a citizen of heaven and a citizen of Rome are the same thing.

Evangelism becomes foreign policy. When the kingdom ceases to be God's kingdom, but God is believed to be blessing the kingdom of a secular state, then to attack another country is to save them from their paganism. It is an act of kindness and is God's will for the entire world to live under the rule of our king, who represents God. This explains the Crusades, the Inquisition, and many of the ugly religious acts of history. It is a holy mission of God to take other countries; if a few people must die, it is worth the quest.

This land is God's land. When the church became defined by geography, this led to the concept of the parish. Everyone living in a certain region, or *parish*, was automatically a member of the true church. It was genetic, automatic, built into the culture and the state. The result was a church that was part Christian, part pagan, all trained in how to relate, so telling the regenerate from the pretenders was nearly impossible and not important. Instead of believers seeing themselves as embattled ones charged with the responsibility to shine light into darkness, evangelism became seen as unneeded. This "cut the nerve" of personal witness and mission.

Thus the church finally broke, and the pathology today in the church of Western Europe clearly illustrates the damage done. Just this last year the Lutheran Church of Sweden officially separated from the state after more than four hundred years. The figurehead of the church did not even believe in God. A church tour of many European countries is a matter of walking through museums and admiring the architecture.

The home of the brave and the land of the free. When seekers come to America to tour the church, they are looking for places where God is at work. We should be thankful that God is at work in some marvelous ways in our land. But more than 80 percent of our churches will be candidates for a quaint church tour if they continue in the present paradigm. American Christendom was fragmented into denominations where the principles of Christendom were applied and are still largely practiced.

The lives of the clergy and the congregants are still very "top down" in the mainline denominations. The infrastructures of religious life, such as mission societies, seminaries, books of order, and lexicons, regulate the practices and teachings of the local congregations. In many of the larger, more historic groups, funding is compulsory and control is still strong with respect to structure. People's minds are not controlled, but the apparatus available to express one's faith and impact the world is controlled.

The parish mentality is still practiced by many mainline denominations. It is unofficially practiced by evangelicals. While mainlines are afflicted with their European past and the early beginnings in this country, evangelicals regularly inflict themselves with such nonsense. As a result many assign regions to their churches and say, "This five-mile radius is covered." Other denominations can invade the radius, but no one from their denomination can enter because there is already "our kind" of church there. There may be one hundred thousand residents in this region, our church may have 125 in attendance, and the combined church attendance of all denominations in the region may be seven thousand, but we won't bring in any more churches because of the insecurity of the pastor and the worry about losing members to the new work. This outlook is evidence that we are so "brain dead" we can't figure out how to have ten distinct ministries to reach the various pockets of people in a given area. It is deadly; it is a wrong; it is Christendom redux.

The primary Christendom relic. You may remember Win Arn's alarming finding that 89 percent of the laity thought the purpose of the church was to care for its members. Many of that 89 percent also believe in a paradigm of the church that is a rusty relic. Lyle Schaller sees this as a major problem facing Great Commission progress:

> Finally, another large cloud hovers over those who define church as Sunday morning and Sunday evening worship, Sunday School, Wednesday evening, loving pastoral care by a long tenured minister married to a saintly wife, vacation Bible school, summer camp, revivals, large crowds at weddings and funerals, and, perhaps, a common nationality or vocational or social class or denominational identity that reinforces cohesion and unity.[9]

The Christendom paradigm is broken. We have a choice: Just let it break, or we can smash it, throw away the mold, and then start over. The fact is that it won't be that easy. You can't just say, "This is wrong, it must go, kill it!" Well-meaning people who are cutting edge in their workplace have a Christendom gravitational pull on their thinking. They think Old World in church and then expound the global village. What will be required is repentance, born of the Spirit of God and applied to both individual and corporate life. It will necessitate the introduction of alternatives in a loving and supportive environment by leaders who understand both Scripture and organizational ethos. It will require mature leaders who are willing to "die to self" in order to live again (John 12:24–25).

Blocked Renewal

Barrier Three: *Denominations are systemically blocking renewal rather than empowering it.* The key word here is systemic: *sis´temik* "of the bodily system as a whole" according to the *New Little Oxford Dictionary*. I am not talking about intention or the personal desire of leaders. If anything, denominational leaders want change more than anyone else. The blocking of renewal comes in the system in which the leaders live and operate. I know of no greater frustration than that of denominational leaders who want to change the system.

A friend recently asked me, as a former denominational executive, how much of our budget went to meeting the needs of churches.

I spoke of the millions of missions dollars and the effective way we helped our churches send missionaries and fulfill their desire to do the Great Commission.

"That doesn't count," he challenged. "There are many parachurch missions that could and do replace that function. What do you actually provide that makes them better churches?" He said that the churches that wanted to send missionaries already had the vision and were already motivated. In particular, he wanted to know about U.S. ministries of denominations and how they served their U.S. churches. I spoke of assisting urban pastors, holding youth conferences, providing medical insurance and retirement for pastors, and loaning churches money for construction of facilities. His interrogation continued until we focused on how the national church, not district or regional bodies, made the churches more fruitful. He said most of our services were basic and expected, that they were passive, since they usually responded to churches wanting to take care of their pastor or build because they were growing. His penetrating analysis was trying to uncover any cause and effect between national initiatives and improved local congregations. In the end he concluded that it would be generous to claim that 25 percent of our budget went to serving the churches. He may not be right, but such a person is a Christian lay leader, and that is his

His penetrating analysis was trying to uncover any cause and effect between national initiatives and improved local congregations.

perspective. Not all, but most lay leaders would agree with him.

I see more of a connection between denominational help and local church growth than my friend did. But his questions forced me to ask, "What are denominations for?" "Why do so many church leaders question their relevance?" Some even speak of the death of denominations and say that we are living in a postdenominational world.

A very caring lay leader approached me at a regional conference where I was speaking. He asked, "Can you tell me why we need a regional director and office? I cannot think of one thing they do for my church. They just ask for money." Why do many lay leaders wonder, *Why do we even need those people at headquarters, when they don't do anything but ask for money?* I know denominations have much less impact than they could have. In many cases their reputations for irrelevance have been earned. Too many would say, "They take from us; they give very little."

What Are Denominations For?

Why is this important? Peter Drucker tells us that the purpose of organizations is to empower ideas. That is what a denomination is for, to empower, to unleash thousands of people and churches with the single idea of fulfilling God's assigned mission on this planet and for this time. Denominations are to inspire and mobilize congregations around their common beliefs and passions, to provide the kind of direction that keeps that vision alive and moving forward. They are to stay close to the needs and quests of local congregations and dedicate themselves as servant-leaders to champion the cause of the commonly held responsibilities of each church.

The vast majority of churches in America are influenced by their denominational history and doctrine. Pastors are very much tied to denominations through ordination, insurance, retirement, and placement. Their careers are very much connected to them. For that reason, denominational

77

leaders still have the best opportunity to have more lasting impact on the majority of churches than any existing movement or megachurch. The real question is, *Will denominational leaders take advantage of their influence? The opportunity is there for the taking.*

Most denominations started for good reasons. Their genesis was and continues to be high-minded, the intentions lofty. They wanted to do together what individual congregations could not do separately. They could mobilize resources, including missionaries. There needed to be a way of credentialing clergy, pooling resources to plant churches, and creating colleges and seminaries to educate their children and the clergy. Another task that remains vital is the preservation of doctrinal distinctives, to protect the theological moorings of the movement. These represent the core of what denominations have been for. There is very little disagreement about that. The difficulty is what they have become.

Missional Neglect

The decline of denominations is linked to missional neglect. It was assumed that people would respect and love the institution and that the churches would self-perpetuate the apologetic for the national body. This was true when the body was small and in many cases ethnically based. But as growth came and constituents were Americanized, those safeguards went away.

In an effort to remain relevant, national leaders embraced a government paradigm. This represents one of the greatest encroachments of secular society on the church. The government taxes us and redistributes the wealth. It regulates our lives and offers a variety of services. If the rules are broken, the government takes punitive action.

Denominations have behaved in much the same way. The degree of politicalization is based on polity and how authority is accessed and used. This is the power of culture, but there is a real difference between that culture and the people who work in it. Church leaders face the same conflicts and frustrations as political reformers.

Lyle Schaller describes the conflict:

> A fourth cloud is over those sincere, deeply committed, and loyal denominational officials who (a) agree that reform is overdue, (b) are completely open to change, (c) find themselves frustrated because they are working a system that is designed to perpetuate the past, and (d) are unable to identify the person or agency that has the authority and the responsibility to initiate change. These leaders are the victims of systemic gridlock.[10]

I know executives in many denominations, and they are accurately described by Schaller. Many challenge for change, but if keys are not found to unlock the proper doors of change, frustration sets in and then turns to disillusionment. Those called to lead the national church wrestle with, "Why do we exist?" "Where do we need to go and how do we get there?" If only the pastors and congregants knew that denominational leaders agonize over these issues more than they, then the following perceptions would die. Unfortunately these perceptions are alive.

That is what a denomination is for, to empower, to unleash thousands of people and churches with the single idea of fulfilling God's assigned mission on this planet and for this time.

Churches Feel Used

Pastors and lay leaders perceive that denominations think that churches should fund the denominations and that they have an obligation to do so, even if it doesn't make sense. Pastors are also required to support denominational causes, often crafted by out-of-touch executives. The churches are asked to follow the decrees or suggestions handed down from the "holy city."

I don't know one denominational leader who wants to be thought of that way or who wants to use the churches for denominational gain. But many pastors and laypeople have

Pastors are increasingly conflicted concerning their denominations, and funding of denominations is growing more difficult.

these perceptions. As a result, pastors are increasingly conflicted concerning their denominations, and funding of denominations is growing more difficult.

Irrelevance of Service

I remember when I was pastoring, getting wastebaskets full of mail from my denomination's various departments. Everything seemed twenty years old and not very useful. The denominational magazine served only as a newsy review of who was moving where. The articles were not written for me. They were nice "corn on the cob" devotionals targeted to somebody else. I read other periodicals that more adequately addressed my needs.

There were of course many denominational requests for money. I don't mind being asked for money. I do, however, like to be told why giving would advance the kingdom. What difference would it make? I thought "those fellas" at HQ just didn't understand me or what I needed or the world I lived in. I didn't hold it against them. In fact I felt sorry for them. Their jobs were so self-defeating.

A pastor of an independent church approached me during a break in a workshop I was leading. He proceeded to relate to me a fantastic story of when his church attempted to join my denomination. "We asked the district supervisor to come and tell us what it would be like to be a part of your group. When we asked him what advantages there were to being a part of your movement, he thoughtfully paused, then answered, 'You can get great discounts at our bookstore.'" That was when they simply dropped the idea. I don't blame them.

When I took one of those self-defeating jobs, I determined to be relevant. I concluded and still believe that the only purpose of leaders in a national body is to improve the ability of churches to be both faithful and fruitful. During the six years I invested in denominational leadership, I focused on knowing and meeting the needs of pastors. The root of irrelevance is the unwillingness to listen to pastors and then design ways to help them fulfill their dreams.

Wasting Resources

There is a prevailing notion among local church skeptics that there is much wastefulness in creaky old organizations. Denominations are about as creaky as it gets, and many wonder how so much money can be spent with such little results. This attitude is a blend of the cynicism built into American life via our political system and the truth that there is precious little to show for the money given.

The Builder generation gives to buildings and to national programs for the sake of loyalty and survival of what they love. Boomers believe that if it can't be paid for, let it die. Boomers are giving less and less to denominational initiatives. Some studies demonstrate that the lack of loyalty on the part of Boomers hurts giving in general by 92 percent.[11]

The Boomers, Busters, and younger generations must be shown why giving is important, and it must be demonstrated that giving adds value to their lives and their local congregations. The perception of waste comes when congregants see no discernible relevant results. When they see results, the vague notion of wastefulness goes away.

Weak Leadership

"If you can't really cut it at the local church level, then fail upward. Become a district or national executive." While not widely admitted, this is a common belief among dynamic leaders. Some denominational positions are considered vehicles for easing into retirement. This notion varies greatly from denomination to denomination. There are some in which it is manifestly untrue, but too many examples make the case for those who choose to believe it.

When an organization profiles their leadership positions as pastors serving pastors, or some kind of pastoral-care vehicle, it is setting itself up to staff the cause with chaplains—very nice people who are not leaders. Denominations need leaders, and the role of a national leader is far different from that of a small church pastor. The skill sets are vastly different. What makes a successful pastor can cause misery for everyone at a national assignment.

My experience as a denominational executive meant that I worked with many faithful and caring people. Some of them were "wired" for the assignment, but frankly, many were not. For me, attempting to tackle the imposing mission of helping the church get better was much like entering the National Basketball Association with a team of twelve players: three NBA quality players and nine midgets. The majority of the team were mismatched for the task. This was not their fault; the selection process simply did not match the person to the assignment.

Those of us at the national level had not done a good job of defining exactly why we existed, and our mission had not penetrated the churches and regional bodies enough to make a change in the paradigm—the way we chose leaders. Additionally, the denomination looked for staff whom they could afford, which does not usually include the best candidates. In this case, perception of weak leadership was reality. But it really wasn't *weak* leadership; it was *wrong* leadership. Being in the wrong role doesn't mean you're weak; it means you're a victim of bad thinking and planning.

Can Anything Be Done?

Let's review what is wrong. First, the systemic issues frustrate the denominational leaders themselves. Second, the "grassroots" people perceive that the whole enterprise is in decline, irrelevant, and needs to be radically changed. As long as these barriers exist, there is little hope that the majority of churches in America that are tied to denominational culture can be good stewards of revival.

For denominations the most important questions crying out for answers are: Why do we exist? and, How can we help our churches achieve their dream of significant spiritual impact? Stanley Stuber's work, *How We Got Our Denominations*, points out that the original purpose of the fifteen largest denominations was to protect biblical fidelity. I suppose many of the mainlines have failed in this first responsibility. They have questions, such as, What do we believe? that must precede the two proposed above. But for theologically conservative groups, the above questions focus on what Peter Drucker calls the "what is your business?" question.

Drucker's Social Sector

Peter Drucker believes the future of the denominations is in the social sector, which does not involve taxation, rule making, or providing goods and services at or above cost that is found in the government or business sectors. "The primary focus of the third sector is to change people, to create human health and well-being."[12] This would include the following:

1. Planting new churches
2. Resourcing existing congregations
3. Challenging and strategizing with congregational leaders about new ministries that meet new needs for new generations
4. Improving the quality and relevance of present ministries
5. Encouraging congregations to follow a systems approach to ministry instead of collecting a group of separate and unrelated programs[13]

Three Major Considerations

David Schmidt, in his work *Choosing to Live*, names three major areas that need to be considered for change. These are the three realms of the denominational product: cause, community, and corporation.

Cause is the compelling idea or conviction that mobilizes a group of people. The issues here are, What is the denominational cause? and, What value do we get back for aligning with it?

Community is where people, because of a sense of affinity based on values, geography, ethnicity, or interest, band together. The issue here is, What benefit do we get from putting the denomination's name on our sign?

Corporation means that membership in an organization yields certain benefits. The issue here is, What is the value of being legally bound to the denomination?[14]

Drucker and Schmidt have organized the issues or sectors that need to be addressed. Schmidt later says *systemic problems are solved by systemic solutions.* Just as the best local churches learn how to process their people and understand their product, so denominations must learn their product and then create a cohesive system that has been changed systemically. Otherwise, renewal will only be rhetoric and window dressing. It will be like repainting and redecorating the *Titanic.*

Throw Out What's Ineffective

The only thing sacred is the biblical fidelity of the organization. Everything else must be negotiable. We don't want to throw out the baby—the biblical moorings—with the bathwater—environment or denominational ethos (traditions and customs surrounding beliefs). The bucket represents the container or structures that hold both the beliefs and customs of the group. We do need to throw out the bathwater and the bucket. Why do we exist? This question and the related one—How can we help our churches achieve their dream of significant spiritual impact?—should rule the entire change process.

> *The least-talked-about factor in restoring relevance and impact to denominational bodies is the courageous leadership required.*

Change will require time, patience, and serious courage on the part of leaders. I have sat around the conference table discussing the opposition we could expect if certain changes were made. It is as though there were a terrifying army of traditional ghosts who would haunt the change process. All many denominational leaders need is for a few ghosts to yell "BOO!" and they run for cover. "It must not be of God." "It's too hard!" "People will call me names and question my integrity."

That is right, expect it. A person is not only known by having the right friends but by having the right enemies.

The least-talked-about factor in restoring relevance and impact to denominational bodies is the courageous leadership required to charge the hill and keep going even when the battle does not seem winnable. There will be times when it looks as if the "body count" is too high, but taking the hill will be worth it in the end.

The most widely recognized World War II monument is soldiers raising the flag of victory on the small South Pacific island of Iwo Jima. It was a bloody battle. But a desolate and seemingly meaningless piece of rock became sacred to Americans because of the great courage displayed there. It was part of a no-win battle. It seemed as though the loss of life was too great. But Americans determined that this was a hill to die on.

Is any price too high to pay if it will serve as a redemption to relevance and advancing the kingdom? We must select our hills carefully, but there are ones worthy of our sacrifice. For denominational leaders, leaving the ineffective way behind is one of them.

What Difference Can Denominations Make?

What makes denominations a barrier also makes them a vital link to revival and reformation of the church. Denominations still hold sway over most of the churches in America. This may not be true of the megachurches, but it is certainly true of most other churches and pastors. Pastors' careers are tied to denominational leaders, and their ability to be placed in a church in which they are credentialed is largely at the mercy of the denominational system. The gatekeepers of the churches are the same pastors; thus the relationship between the local, regional, and national gatekeepers is vital. If they sense they are on a team, working and helping one another to succeed, then in that unity and vision they can strategize, change, and move forward powerfully.

Trust and unity lead to productive communication, which leads to truth. When people start telling each other the truth about needs, progress results. When pastors believe that the national and regional leaders' main drive and passion are to see them succeed, then multiplied fruitfulness and the reaping of a great harvest appear on the horizon. It can happen. We pray that it does happen, and unless it does, many will miss the joy of fruitfulness. I can't think of a greater waste, a greater sorrow, a greater tragedy.

Break Through the Barriers

God continues to send his power for spiritual awakening. He has already provided the power that is needed. The crucial question is, Will the church prepare to be good stewards? This in part means a willingness to break through the barriers.

On an individual basis: Are we willing to consider changing local church paradigms in order to restore the cutting edge and get out of the margins of society? This is done by investing in training people as disciples and letting the Holy Spirit, rather than our limiting subculture, shape them and their callings. Let Scripture define what it means to be spiritual.

On a local church basis: Are we willing to reorganize corporately? Are we willing to move from a collection of unrelated ministries that are all equal and built around meeting our needs? Will we move to a more intentional focus on reaching the world around us and in the process meet our own needs?

On a national basis: Are we willing to revisit the purpose and transform our organizations from the top-down organizations that churches support for the purpose of advancing a national agenda to a servant-leader model that helps its churches mobilize to reach their dreams and, in the process, the world?

The barriers will come down when we repent and determine to have our rhetoric match our actions. That is when we will hear those beautiful words promised by our Lord. "Then you will call, and the LORD will answer; you will cry for help, and he will say: Here am I" (Isa. 58:9).

The Nature of Revival 5

People have many things in common, but what sets us apart from one another is our looks and personalities. Each of us possesses a common nature, and a personality that is easygoing or outgoing or intense or high strung or some other description. Revivals, like people, have common characteristics that can be indexed and thus be given the label *revival*. But each expression of God jump-starting his church has its own personality. It is one thing to define the intentional move of God on the church, but quite another to discuss what it is like to live with revival.

I can say that strong families are vital to the rebuilding of the moral fiber of our nation. But that does not touch on the distinctive personality of each marriage. Every good relationship finds its way to an acceptable norm that is satisfying to each partner.

For example, I am afflicted with mechanical dyslexia. When I see a plan for a reconstruction project, it makes no sense to me. My wife on the other hand is mechanically gifted; she can build anything. She is a person of vision: She conceptualized elaborate forts for our sons that served as both beds and play areas. She designed them, went to the lumberyard, purchased the materials, returned home, and promptly built two large fort-beds. She recently redesigned our bathroom, knocked out the back wall of the house, replaced it with glass block, put in a new shower and tub, and replumbed it. All I had to do was come home to the prospect of showering surrounded only by glass block! Our relationship has its own distinctive personality. So does each revival.

How God chooses to work with one part of the body of Christ may be very different from how he works with another part.

How God chooses to work with one part of the body of Christ may be very different from how he works with another part. In recent months God has jump-started certain sections of his church. In both Toronto and the Pensacola revivals, he has been at work expressing himself through the distinctive genre of charismatic evangelicals. Not everything done in the name of God is from God. So when God expresses himself in the charismatic genre, not everything that happens finds its origin in him. This is just as true in a revival where many "walk the aisles." Most of those going forward are legitimate, but there will be those just going through the motions. Whether it is going forward, kneeling, lying prostrate on the ground, or jumping up and down like a kangaroo, some responses are generated by God, some by the human flesh.

Certain signs that are very likely to be present in the charismatic version of revival will be absent with Southern Baptists or Episcopalians. God is doing the same thing but he is doing it differently based on human choices, understanding, and traditions. Just as God used the differing educational levels and grammatical skills of Paul, Mark, and Matthew to compose Scripture, he will work through his church, honoring the differences and the temperament of each member.

Progress

God sends revival to make progress in his quest to seek and save that which is lost (Luke 19:10). The church possesses a sense of progress that is built around new church starts and growth of existing congregations. God is more focused on adding new children to his family. While these foci are not mutually exclusive, God's purpose in sending generous supplies of his power is to further the pristine form of his mission. The church's sense of mission is polluted with all the vulgarities of human nature.

Progress Is Not Uniform

God makes progress through the realities of the human condition. Therefore progress is not uniform or constant. Any progress is like the incoming tide: Each wave is revival going forward, receding, then followed by another. God makes the waves. He is in charge of their size and how far the tide comes in. Each new surge of revival has its own characteristics and direction, but its nature is revival. James Burns describes it,

> We can see God's wisdom. Revivals are necessary to push humankind to higher planes. If progress were uniform, with all aspects of life improving at once, advancement would be so slow that life would stagnate. There would be no high hopes, no eager rush forward. Progress would be imperceptible—and men and women, robbed of aspirations, would give up the fight.[1]

I will never forget that night on the basketball team in Brownsville, Texas, when I scored sixteen out of eighteen field goals, most of them from today's three-point range. I was seven out of eight from the free throw line. The only reason I didn't score fifty was that we were well ahead, so I didn't play the last ten minutes. I was in what athletes call "the zone." The basket was twice as big, my rhythm was perfect, my confidence soared to new levels, and I was ready to shoot as soon as we crossed the midcourt area. In the years I played basketball, I had a few nights in "the zone" but most nights I was mortal, which led to a 50 percent field goal shooting percentage for the year and a 22-point-a-game average.

The ebb and flow of human personality makes living "in the zone" impossible. The equilibrium is in God's hands. Human life does not move with precision; the wills of men and women, with all their inconstancy, have impact. God not only moves with the personality of human flow, he controls the flow of his power to move men and women forward. It would simply be too intense to live life in the zone or always at a level of revival. This is the reason that we speak of mountaintop experiences and we also speak of going through valleys of difficulty. Trying to always live on a high plane violates the cycles of life.

Every week on Dick Clark's *American Bandstand* the dancers rated a new record. If they liked the song, they often would say, "I liked the beat." The beat is the fundamental percussion and rhythm that governs the intensity and speed of the music.

God designed the cycles of life, beginning with the solar system, for the rotation of the earth, night and day, the ocean tides, and their relationship to the moon and the seasons. Add to that the human need to sleep, exercise, contemplate, celebrate, be intense, mellow out . . . this all is God's doing. So it would only make sense that God, who creates the beat, would work through the cycles that he has designed. That means that Finney's idea that we could always live in a state of revival is at odds with all of God's creation.

God works in spurts. He moves us forward by creating a highly charged environment, then like the tide, it recedes. But even the tide makes progress in receding, if the tide is moving in. So if we are moving in the right direction,

90

progress is even being made when we drop back or relax the intensity of activity. When the tide recedes, it is gathering momentum for the future waves.

I think that Christians often misunderstand how God works, and feel as if they have lost the Spirit or power when the emotion is gone. A receding of emotion or activity after a powerful experience does not mean that we are less spiritual or that God is less present. Much of what God does is emotional: This can be anything from healing and outward manifestations to many people quietly turning their lives over to God. But when the meetings are done and the lights are out, some think, *God has departed, because I don't feel him anymore.* They go on to lament, "Why can't it last? This is the way it ought to be all the time!" They are dead wrong. This is poor theology and leads to unneeded expectations and disappointment.

> *Revival has its place in the church and the Christian life. But it is a small place and it is rare.*

If we are to believe the Bible, God is present in us at all times (Rom. 8:9–11; Col. 2:9–10; 1 John 1:7–9). During seasons when we walk in the power of the Spirit, disappointment plays a minor role. The goal of God sending a greater measure of his Spirit is to move us closer to him and his agenda for the world. Rather than trying to maintain the energy of the revival moment or event, we need to transform that energy into lasting godly living and fruitfulness in everyday life. Everyday life is lived at a different energy level than a special event.

When a college campus is struck with revival, often classes are let out for several days, and people are caught up in the powerful sweep of God's Spirit. If that were normal, classes would never start again, learning would end, people would stop paying tuition, parents would pull their children from that school, the faculty would lose their jobs, and the college would close. You would rightly say, "How absurd." But it is no more absurd than to think that the normal Christian experience is to be lived at a revival high.

What follows revival on a college campus is a return to normal life patterns, yet with a renewed purpose as to the goals for attending classes and taking exams. The work of God's Spirit to help students renew a commitment to the daily grind of right living, studying, and working hard is no less spectacular than what took place in the chapel.

Revival has its place in the church and the Christian life. But it is a small place and it is rare. We thank God for what he has done and what he will do to revive his church. But revival as a way of life is what is needed as normal Christians learn to walk with God daily in a consistent but unspectacular way.

> *Revival, like crisis and pain, is a catalyst for acceleration to get us to our destination on time.*

God's Schedule

Is God on schedule? The answer to that question depends on the level at which you want to answer. When we think of God's sovereignty and his redemptive time clock, we would need to say yes. Scripture speaks of the "fullness of time" concept. We are also told that when the gospel is preached to everyone, he will return (Matt. 24:14). Would God like to rescue the world faster? My holy hunch is yes, but he has chosen a different approach. The redemptive plan is connected to the church. He turned over the execution of that plan to the apostles in the upper room and in turn it was passed on to us (Matt. 28:18–20; John 13–16; Acts 1:8; 2 Cor. 5:18–21).

In the ebb and flow of human church history, periodically God infuses the church with wider and greater power to move us forward faster to compensate for lost time and ground. The reasons for this, of course, is human nature and the disobedience of the church. God doesn't really have a plan B. What he has is the rod of discipline and the offer of forgiveness and a new start. So God is at work, he is on time, and historic revival is a crucial part of working for final redemption. Revival, like crisis and pain, is a catalyst for acceleration to get us to our destination on time.

Signs of a Coming Revival

Any weatherman worth his electronic pointer has and can read the remarkable Doppler radar. This new form of radar is now commonplace in major television markets. It not only tells you where storms are and how fast they are moving but provides precise information on the composition of the moisture and its ferocity. This system provides ample warning to the public so they can make sensible preparations for a coming storm and has led to the saving of many lives.

It is common for a very excited weatherman armed with his high-tech pointer to say, "There is a strong warm front moving fast out of the Gulf of Mexico. There is a lot of moisture in this major storm. And look at this, an Alberta Clipper sailing out of Canada with some very cold air." He raises his voice, "Do you see what I see? These two fronts will smash into each other over Saint Louis! Saint Louis," he sternly stares into the camera, "Batten down the hatches. You can expect over a foot of snow by Wednesday afternoon!"

Predicting revivals is not an exact science. They come less frequently than snowstorms and are more difficult to foresee. There are, however, a few signs that can help us anticipate them. If one has his head up and observes what is taking place in the evangelical world, it would be reasonable to consider that God is ready to infuse his church yet again with a major jolt of power.

Spiritual Dryness

The strongest visual image of spiritual dryness is Ezekiel's vision of the dry bones coming to life. In other texts, water has been one of the symbols of the Holy Spirit's work in bringing new life to a dry spiritual environment.

Almost every major revival has been preceded by an environment of spiritual desert or dead orthodoxy. Present culture is a combination of superficial orthodoxy and a deep-seated multicultural spiritual pluralism that leads to a shapeless spirituality. The spiritual prayer of our culture is addressed "to whom it may concern." Western culture is overall a parched spiritual land.

It seems as though God has a limit on how long he will allow his church to be nonproductive. He focuses on seeking and saving, which imply intentionality and aggression and requires spiritual passion. So spiritual dryness is a given as a prerequisite. When some other signs are added, then it can be surmised that God is ready to act.

A Unity Front

A major change in the face of American evangelicalism is the coming together of denominational leaders to work for the common interest of the evangelization of the nation. The apex of this movement is Mission America, an outgrowth of the Lausanne movement. Their motto is "The Gospel for every person, a church for every Christian." Mission America's strategy is to pray that God will bring together various parts of the church in the cities of America. Typically, several denominational leaders, mission agency directors, and local pastors develop a citywide strategy. It seems that everyone from Southern Baptists to Episcopalians can agree on two things: that God will pour out his Spirit on our land, and that the Great Commission will be fulfilled. Around this common desire God is bringing his body together. Jesus prayed, "I have given them the glory that you gave me, that they may be one as we are one: I in them and you in me. May they be brought to complete unity to let the world know that you sent me and have loved them even as you have loved me" (John 17:22–24).

Almost every major revival has been preceded by an environment of spiritual desert or dead orthodoxy.

When the church unites, it becomes much more powerful. The reason is simple, as Jesus prayed: "By this all men will know that you are my disciples, if you love one another. . . . to let the world know that you sent me" (John 13:35; 17:23).

94

The most powerful way the church can touch the world is for us to love one another and to present a united front to the world. Jesus claimed that unity will communicate that God sent his Son and the church is the result. This does not mean that we lay aside our doctrinal distinctives or traditions, unless they keep us from obeying God. Extreme separatistic, spirited people work against the unity and limit the power that God wants to release through them. Refusing to work with others, who are basically orthodox but differ on some marginal doctrine, is sin. It is wrong because it hurts that particular part of the church, limiting its outreach. It also cheats the rest of the church of the unique contribution that part of the body can give to the cause.

It seems that everyone from Southern Baptists to Episcopalians can agree on two things: that God will pour out his Spirit on our land, and that the Great Commission will be fulfilled.

I am a graduate of Oral Roberts University. I would not, however, be considered a charismatic. I grew up Wesleyan, attended a charismatic university, graduated from a dispensational seminary, and am ordained in the Evangelical Free Church. I have theological opinions but I would be considered a moderate on controversial issues of theology. I simply am not arrogant enough to think that my interpretation of Scripture on fuzzy issues is always right. Therefore, I am willing to work with anyone who believes in the Triune God and believes Scripture to be inspired of God. Issues such as how or when people are baptized are denominational distinctives, certainly not reasons to refuse to work together.

When I graduated from college, I joined Athletes in Action, the sports arm of Campus Crusade for Christ. I was raising my support and one day was lunching with a wealthy businessman who wanted to support sports ministry. He agreed with Campus Crusade's commitment to the Great Commission and spoke very highly of the Athletes in Action work. I was really enjoying my lunch. He was paying, plus he was going to support me with fifty dollars a month. In

1969 this was a lot of money. Then it happened. He asked, "Where did you go to college, Bill?"

"Oral Roberts University," I proudly announced.

"Oral Roberts is a quack," he spit. He called for the check and told me that he would have nothing to do with me.

That was a shocker. It was the start of an education for me in how utterly parochial and closed minded well-meaning Christian leaders can be. I found this attitude so foul that I committed right then and there I would never become like that. This kind of attitude still gives me the creeps. It is because it comes from a very bad place; it is the spirit of separatism that is devilish in origin.

The most powerful way the church can touch the world is for us to love one another and to present a united front to the world.

The Spirit of Christ is the spirit of unity, and he prayed for us and commanded us to work together on the big-ticket items. Unity will release great power because it is a prerequisite for revival and it makes the church a much better steward of what God wants to do through us.

A Prayer Front

The main instrument God uses to develop the unity front is prayer. The prayer movement today has three tributaries. The first is the Concerts of Prayer movement, which focuses its efforts in the laity and the local church. Dr. David Bryant has been greatly used of God in leading the church into a widespread movement of prayer.

The second tributary is the Pastors Prayer Summits started by International Renewal Ministries. Dr. Joe Aldrich and Dr. Terry Dirks were the men God used to bring together thousands of pastors around the nation, and now the world, to pray for revival and spiritual renewal.

The third tributary is led by Dr. Bill Bright, founder of Campus Crusade for Christ. He has brought together major leaders of denominations and mission agencies to pray and fast together.

The Concerts of Prayer bring together laity from churches. The Pastors Prayer Summits bring pastors together from various denominations, and Dr. Bright's prayer and fasting sessions have brought national leaders together. The barriers of ego, fear of revealing our weaknesses, doctrinal differences, and a host of other fleshly pathologies evaporate in a context of prayer and fasting. All three tributaries are crucial in

The Spirit of Christ is the spirit of unity, and he prayed for us and commanded us to work together on the big-ticket items.

that they cover the entire church and its gatekeepers. Add to this the growing activity in our nation's capital around the National Day of Prayer, and God seems to be at work in bringing his people together.

I remember well the process I went through at a forty-eight-hour prayer and fasting session. Being a Christian leader and one who walks with God, I had no serious challenges the first evening, praying with other people I had just met. The first evening peeled away the first layer of defense. The second day, however, I had to confess my sins of over-work and being too dedicated to the cause. Classically at such events we repent of our schedules and all the other sins we are so proud of.

Since we were stuck there for three days, we started talking about our fears, about the systemic sins such as attitudes about other groups, both denominational and racial. At the midpoint of day two I had emptied myself of all uncleanness that I could identify. Then God began to minister to me in a fresh and new way that I had never known before. I can only say that I felt united to those around me and felt them to be kindred spirits. When these barriers are broken, we begin to build unity. Then we can share resources to create a stronger church and reach out to others. *This is a crucial process to understand. Prayer breaks barriers and then builds unity, and the unity means we are willing to share resources in order to achieve shared vision.*

97

Surf's Up

When a storm is raging at sea and is moving toward land, the surf gets big. The phrase "surf's up" has been a part of beach cultures for decades. The weatherman says prospects are good for major surf, so students take their surfboards, waxed and ready, to school, and some adults take them to work. Surfers can't make waves, they can't control the size of waves, but they can hope for and be ready for the big waves. When the call goes out, they grab their boards and hightail it to the beach. A lot of practice on normal waves prepares the surfer for those special rides on the big waves.

I believe the surf's up spiritually. We have a major unity front that is about to collide with a prayer front that will create a great storm. The waves are getting bigger, and we have the responsibility to be ready. God has brought us to a point of expectancy via prayer and unity. We are ready to share resources and work together. This will release great power because Jesus promised it would. Be ready. (I will discuss what it means to be ready in the reformation section of the book.)

Prophets

Every movement requires chosen leaders. I will call them lowercase prophets, since they do not possess the same standing as the Isaiahs, Jeremiahs, or Joels (about whom there was nothing minor). Normally these leaders can't explain why they are so focused on one segment of God's work; they can only tell you that God has given them a special passion and interest. Generally they have departed from the normal pattern of being pastors, teachers, missionaries, or denominational leaders.

Every movement of ideas requires a body of literature and focused fanatics in the Churchillian definition: "A fanatic is someone who can't change his mind and won't change the subject." These leaders don't seem to mind being "labeled" or placed in a category.

When I was considering devoting all my time to helping the church return to its disciple-making roots, a well-respected leader told me that I would be labeled *discipleship*. Indeed that has happened. It is part of the price of focus that people will consider your portfolio very limited.

Not only are *you* categorized, the common understanding of what you are doing is also limited. Discipleship for example has falsely been miniaturized by the church to be just another activity. Discipleship is the process of following Jesus in the context of accountability in the church. Disciple making is much broader and includes all dimensions of church life and the Great Commandment and the Great Commission. Making disciples is not just one of the things a church does, it is *what* the church does.

The person God enlists to speak to his church must be able to clarify, to be the master of the obvious, because the church constantly forgets the obvious directions God issued—to be healthy and reach the world. These are the Great Commandment and the Great Commission.

The Role of Prophets

Most prophets don't have anything new to say. Guts and focus are much more useful than creativity. God has raised up many in our contemporary church. Billy Graham, Bill Bright, David Bryant, and Joe Aldrich are examples.

God raises up prophets on the revival side of the equation and also on the reformation side. On the revival side those of the last decade's prayer movement have been crucial, along with those of the Promise Keepers movement. But as this book's thesis proposes, the voices on the reformation side are of equal importance. The revival side spokespersons generate the beginnings of God at work by helping the church understand the issues and the need for reflection, repentance, and a returning to the first things. The

> *Making disciples is not just one of the things a church does, it is what the church does.*

99

reformation speakers point out how to be good stewards of what God is doing and how to extend the "shelf life" of revival.

We have wasted much of what God has done because we have divided these two issues in our minds and in our practice. It has been a costly error to call revival the spiritual work and then to consider the changing of church structure an unspiritual or managerial function. If you don't think church structure is a spiritual battleground, interview some pastors. It is absolutely false to think that revival alone will melt away thorny issues, such as the role of the pastor, the role of the laity, and the removal of traditional structure, which impedes outreach and brings great disillusionment to the church.

Restating the Message

The truth does not change, but our comprehension of it does. It needs to be restated regularly to the church from different angles with a new vocabulary. Words are like coins that we daily hold in our hands but don't examine often. The only time we carefully examine money is when it is freshly printed or minted. Then we may take a fresh look at what we commonly ignore.

I attended a church where I enjoyed the people and the pastor. I held the pastor in high esteem, and he was a good speaker. Many people in the church considered him a great teacher. However, I had problems staying with him in his sermons. This confused me. He had passion, his sermons were well crafted, and I agreed with what he said, yet I was bored. After some prayer and talking to my wife, it became clear what was going on. He was thirty years older than I, and most of the people to whom he ministered were older than I. He was using church clichés and language from his generation. His words didn't have the force and precision to cut through the cultural veil that separated us. James Burns observes, "In spiritually dead times, preachers continue to use the old words. Once so full of power, now they have no impact."[2]

Language has changed dramatically in the last thirty years. Certain pulpit jargon has become so hackneyed that it is even heard on *Saturday Night Live*. If we want people to hear, we must bring the message to life by restating the truth with great passion and in a language they understand.

Before the Reformation, the doctrine of justification by faith had ceased to exist. Methods and practices of the church so dominated people's minds that when they read Paul's writings,

If you don't think church structure is a spiritual battleground, interview some pastors.

they could not see the doctrine there. Similarly the contemporary church is blind to the most basic of truths. *Invest in developing people. They become motivated and creative. Then you effectively reach the world around you, and your congregation grows.* These truths are obvious and need to be stated in a powerful and passionate way.

When I had written *The Disciple-Making Pastor* I submitted the manuscript to various publishers. Many turned it down with the comment, "This is not new; everybody knows about equipping the saints." Most church leaders have heard of and are familiar with the concept. But most don't know how to break out of their crusty paradigms and do it. That is why I am committed to the mission of helping churches understand the meaning and the means of becoming disciple making and bearing fruit to make the church a good place to be.

Postmodern Revival

In an article titled "Spiritual Revival 1980s-Style" columnist Henry Mitchell wrote, "So of course we have once more a great American spiritual [is it the third, or the fifth, or the hundredth?] revival. Which is fine with me as long as I've figured out what is meant by spiritual. It means to be a slob as usual and let God rain down the dollars."[3] This skeptical statement reflects the general cynicism of culture watchers to the possibility of a culturally transforming revival.

101

James Davidson Hunter, a Christian and sociologist weighs in on the same subject: "A third great awakening, or second Protestant reformation as it has been called with the same amount of influence as the first and second great awakening in America or as the original Protestant reformation is a virtual sociological, not to mention legal, impossibility under the present conditions of modernity."[4] Both writers have addressed differently the same problem. Hunter speaks to the new cultural construct called postmodernism. Os Guinness describes this construct:

> Where modernism was a manifesto of human self-confidence and self-congratulation, postmodernism is a confession of modesty, if not despair. *There is no truth, only truths. There are no principles, only preferences. There is no grand reason, only reasons. There is no privileged civilization (or culture, beliefs, norms, and styles). . . . There is no universal justice, only interests and the competition of interest groups. . . . There is no simple reality or any grand objectivity of universal, detached knowledge. . . .* post modernism is . . . an extreme form of relativism.[5]

Guinness goes on to note, "If post modernism is correct, we cannot even aspire after truth."[6]

Mitchell speaks of the superficial, selfish, nonimpactful nature of contemporary revival. Such renewal has no impact because it is largely without substance. (This returns us to an earlier section on Isaiah 5 and the serious disconnection between saying and doing the revival ritual without its impacting behavior.)

Mitchell's attitude is really an expression of what Hunter states as the reason for a widespread revival's not taking place. This is what Lesslie Newbigin calls "the acids of modernity."

Fire Walls, Not Fans

Billy Graham is respected by virtually anyone with a normal brain. Even talk-show host Larry King ended an hourlong interview with Graham by saying, "Billy Graham, what a man." Graham is greatly loved by Christians around the world, and we pay attention to what he says. His reflections on the church and his life are of special interest.

Recently he lamented that none of his crusades had transformed a city or society, like those of Finney, Moody, or Sunday. He was speaking of areas where taverns were closed, ladies of the evening went out of business, where the touch of God reached the halls of government and the ivy-covered walls of the university. The reason for Mr. Graham's observation is the difference of the single worldview

> *Modernity has created fire walls to keep the flames of God's working partitioned off.*

society of one hundred years ago and the moral confusion in contemporary society caused by the acids of modernity. It is simply a different world. Modernity has created fire walls to keep the flames of God's working partitioned off.

Graham's observation and Hunter's reasons for thinking that widespread revival is an impossible proposition can be explained by a flashback to my childhood. I grew up in Indianapolis, Indiana, in the 1950s. Ike was president, and we had two channels on our black-and-white TV. If you were lucky you could walk your girlfriend to school and carry her books. We started the school day with prayer and the pledge of allegiance. I got my hair cut down at the corner barbershop for twenty-five cents. I attended, with my grandparents, the Northside Pilgrim Holiness Church, where we were blessed with simple, clear-cut choices about heaven and hell. Twice a year we had scheduled revivals that would be two weeks in duration.

When revival broke out in our church, there was a very good chance that it would spread throughout the community. The primary reason was that our community had a singular worldview. My Little League coach, my homeroom teacher, the principal of my school, the barber, the pastor, the mayor, and government officials agreed on right and wrong. The result was that major institutions of society and the popular culture fanned the flames of what God was doing at a

103

local church. Once a week my school class marched over to a local church for religious education at taxpayers' expense.

Contemporary culture does not fan the flames of spiritual renewal. It serves as properly coded fire walls to partition one segment of society from another. Hunter's point is that we have moved from freedom of religion to freedom *from* religion. Government is no longer encouraging religion; it is no longer neutral; it is politely hostile to religious expression in public life.

Culture is no longer an advocate of religion, which makes renewal more difficult. Multiculturalism is simply a product of postmodernism because it teaches that all religions and cultures are morally equal. This places Christians in the unenviable position of being intolerant and religious bigots for taking the position of Christianity's being exclusively true. So we find ourselves in a nonlinear, nonsequential, self-directed world where truth is up for grabs.

> *It is not enough for a large group of already Christian people to "get blessed," to hear from God and call it revival, without real change.*

Both Guinness and Hunter suggest that for real breakthrough to take place, it must break out of the evangelical cultural closet. It is not enough for a large group of already Christian people to "get blessed," to hear from God and call it revival, without real change. It must affect our Christian lifestyles in such a dramatic way that we are significantly distinctive and live consistently with our beliefs. The combination of belief in the truth and living out that truth is the most penetrating of apologetics. To transform culture, revival must reach various levels of cultural authority and then public policy. Enough moral passion to transform people and the vision to reform the church and evangelicalism as a whole is what is needed.

A New Look

Whatever postmodern revival looks like, it will surprise most of us. It certainly will not look like what we have read and heard about from the past. To expect it to be something like the First or Second Great Awakenings would be a great mistake. I hear many talk about revival as though it will be like what God has done in the past. Their heart is right, but the image is wrong. We don't want to be duped by what J. I. Packer calls the "romantic fallacy."

> We fall into this when we let ourselves imagine that revival, once it came, would function as the last chapter in a detective story functions—solving all our problems, clearing up all the difficulties that have arisen in the church, and leaving us in a state of idyllic peace and contentment, with no troubles to perplex us any more.[7]

I recommend that we keep our minds open about how God wants to work with us.

If society is partitioned by institutional fire walls, then the church must target each segment. There are examples of this: missions to college students, to athletes, to the military, to the workplace, to government officials, to the entertainment industry, to prisons, to golfers, to coaches, etc. While this may seem to handle the issue, it does not fully address the problem, for most of this work is based on propositional evangelism—presentation of the gospel in cognitive principles alone. At the core, I agree with the passion that drives such efforts. I think humankind's first and greatest need is to be reconciled to the Creator through the redemptive and finished work of the resurrected Lord Jesus Christ. The limitation of many such efforts is that once converted, the new disciples are assimilated into the same evangelical cultural closet that itself is partitioned off from secular society.

This means most of the converts are then discipled into a Christianity that lacks cultural firepower and ethical punch. It is as though the church has been neutered, put into its place. We tend to make disciples that are culturally like us rather than allowing the creativity of the Holy Spirit to radicalize our approach with strategies that penetrate and capture both the minds and hearts of the unreached.

We are the only country in the world that equates being truly Christian with a certain political philosophy. We have a complete list of behaviors that are off limits, regardless of whether or not they can be supported scripturally. Everything from the use of alcohol, dancing, listening to rock music, or watching late-night television is on that list. I am sure the efforts to live unstained lives are well intentioned, even though they usually turn out to be trivial and moralistic. Such rules create barriers between us and those we would like to reach.

The answer is to radically alter our church structures, priorities, and roles to reach the truly unreached. In the process of altering our church paradigms, we must also reprogram our thinking. This means we must *redefine* our roles in the mission, *redesign* the infrastructures of our churches, and then *reassign* the personnel. When this happens the people from the postmodern culture will understand and develop strategies to reach their own culture. The church needs to send out platoons of individuals who are passionately devoted to reaching their own culture. The Builders will reach Builders, Boomers will reach Boomers, Busters will reach Busters, and so on.

Postmodern revival looks like the Promise Keepers movement—a creative work done by the Holy Spirit through a football coach. It employs the common denominator of men to touch families, the secular marketplace, and then the church itself. That is something church leaders could never have thought of and could never have done. History demonstrates that revival usually begins with restless, unsatisfied Christians, working outside the church. This is another example of stepping outside church structure to reach the church. There are thousands if not millions of other culturally congruent ways to reach people. What is necessary is a church repentant and ready to change. It starts with revival and ends with a radically different church, creatively penetrating the world and capturing millions for Jesus Christ.

We know that God is ready for revival, but is the church? Are we ready to take the second part of spiritual awakening seriously? Are we ready to move from revival to reformation?

PART TWO

Reformation

All thinking begins with a pain in the mind.

Lesslie Newbigin

The Starting Line   6

If the contemporary church were infused with power as was the "first church" in the upper room, we would stay in the upper room, put up a banner, and hold meetings. Then we would make a video and raise funds. The first Christians, however, did the most natural thing; they ran into the streets, preaching the gospel in a language people could understand. It took several years before they began to insulate themselves from the people they were commissioned to reach. That is why so much of the New Testament is written in red corrective pencil, because the human condition began to dominate.

The human condition asks the world to come to us. We stay in the hall and ask others to join the party. This is treating revival as the finish line. Our work is done; now invite the world to join us. But God wants us to be active. He wants us to run into the streets of culture and seek and find those whom God has prepared for rescue.

When God sends a special jolt of power and new life to his church, people have transformed attitudes. They are ready to change in habits and in actions. Unfortunately this is where most revivals end. We treat the confession of sins, forgiveness of one another, and the tremendous tales of transformation as the finish line. But it is at this point that we should be asking God what he wants us to do next and committing ourselves to doing it. Now it is time for "fruit in keeping with repentance" (Luke 3:8). This is actually the starting line. We are now ready to "run the race" described in Scripture (1 Cor. 9:24–27; Heb. 12:1–2). It is time to change attitudes, actions, structures, and anything that stands in the way of faithfulness and fruitfulness.

J. I. Packer writes:

To go beyond revival to reformation will require disciplined thinking and doing. Both are painful!

Revival means renewal of life and life means energy. It is true that revival delivers the church from the problems created by apathy and deadness, but it is equally true that revival plunges the church into a welter of new problems created by the torrential overflow of disordered and undisciplined spiritual vitality. . . . the saints are suddenly roused from a state of torpor and lethargy by a new and overwhelming awareness of the reality of spiritual things. . . . they are like sleepers shaken awake and now half blinded by the unaccustomed glare of the sun.[1]

To go beyond revival to reformation will require disciplined thinking and doing. Both are painful!

Going beyond Revival

Applying God's power to reforming the church is the start of real transformation. But frankly the church has not been willing to go far enough. We must be willing to entertain the notion of breaking the Christendom/traditional mold. This will require the kind of thinking Lesslie Newbigin suggests when he speaks of pain in the mind; it will be painful for us to consider and think through the process. But continuing to chase successful models that are really just upgrades with innovative adjustments to the old paradigm will not give us the breakthrough to fruitfulness that is so greatly desired.

Movie Stars or Great Actors?

Most innovative paradigms that are large are chased after by thousands of pastors, but these successes generally are personality driven and work only for the charismatic personality with wide appeal. It is like the difference between a movie star and a great actor.

To be a movie star requires wide international appeal. The person just has a presence or look, an image that millions around the world can relate to. Some great movie stars are average or even poor actors. Some great actors are not movie stars. They make a living, they teach other actors, but they are not major box office attractions. Arnold Schwarzenegger, Sylvester Stallone, and Steven Segal are great movie stars and average actors. Martin Landau, Ned Beatty, and Dennis Hopper are great actors, but don't have the worldwide box office appeal of a major movie star. The renowned Actors Studio in New York City does not train people to be movie stars; they teach people to act.

Seminaries should not be and are not in the business of creating "pastoral stars." They train "great pastors" who for the most part will never lead a large church. Great pastors are thoroughly committed to being faithful and fruitful. They possess rational self-awareness, maximize their strengths, and follow God's plan to coach/equip believers to be effective ministers. They use their special abilities to draw out and empower the full potential of a congregation.

They are committed to reproducing what is reproducible, namely the characteristics of Christ, not personality or style.

Chasing models to duplicate them is the most practiced mistake among church leaders. The many successful models of the church are a gift to the rest of the church. They provide good ideas. They also give hope to the discouraged that God is at work and can do more in their lives.

Saint Elsewhere

As long as this pursuit of what God is doing elsewhere is a pursuit of principles, all is well. This is true because principles can be applied at the right rate of speed that fits a pastor's leadership ability and the church culture. When it's a pursuit of methods, however, trouble crouches at the door. A model is canonized and methodological sainthood is the result. Let's say a pastor attends a conference where he learns about a seeker-sensitive approach to Sunday morning. This approach has worked wonderfully for one church, which has seen thousands come to Christ. The approach includes transforming the Sunday morning service to an outreach event. What people normally think of as Sunday morning worship takes place on Wednesday night. This works well for the church originating the idea, because the leaders started a new church and built in the values from the beginning. But other congregations may struggle with attempts to repeat the first church's success.

The principle of removing needless obstructions from a Sunday service that make visitors feel like outsiders, of making the service behave as an open group *will* work for another congregation. Many churches think their Sunday services are open to the public, when in fact they behave as a closed group. The music, language, and "insider" comments drive seekers away.

The pastor who doesn't discipline himself to extract the workable principle will simply try to cram the method into his very different church culture. This is much like transplanting a monkey heart into a human being. The human experiences a violent, fatal rejection.

When the thrilled pastor returns home to announce that "church" will now be on Wednesday night and Sunday morning will be an outreach service, an unnecessary human sacrifice is offered on the twin altars of tradition and stupidity—the church's tradition, the pastor's stupidity.

We must break the mold to let churches and pastors seek out new ways of doing church that are congruent with Scripture, their culture, and the abilities of the pastoral leadership. This will require a process. The commitment to that process is the starting line for lasting spiritual awakening. That process has three primary dimensions:

Redefine the mission.
Redesign the infrastructure.
Reassign the personnel.

Let me restate our thesis. For spiritual awakening to come to the church, it will require both revival and reformation. Revival provides the energy; reformation provides the application both on a personal and corporate level. Without systemic revival, the impact of personal renewal will be much less and short-lived. So let's get started.

Redefine the Mission   7

Why redefine the mission? Isn't it clear? Doesn't everyone already know the mission is to be good Christians and win the world for Christ?

Most church leaders can say the right words, presenting very noble reasons for their church's existence. But almost without exception they cannot connect their church activities to church goals. The goals are not really goals and the activities are cultural customs. The goals have no precision, no dates for completion, no one assigned to make sure they happen, no built-in accountability. For most congregations, the various activities of church life are undertaken without any fundamental questioning, evaluation, or any meaningful memory of why the activity started.

The Primary Objective

Marriage, the most fundamental of relationships, reveals the reason to revisit the mission. Our first family car was a '58 Buick station wagon. Its special feature, besides its bright green color, was that every time you hit a big bump the hood would pop up and the tailgate would drop open. When my wife, Jane, and I launched out from the Midwest to California, all our possessions fit into the back of the wagon. We borrowed $250 from Jane's brother and risked everything in that Buick for Christ.

Life was simple, our focus was clear: reach the world and use the gifts that God had given us to do so.

Jane keeps count of the twenty-seven times we have moved in the last twenty-eight years of marriage. Thankfully eighteen of those were in the first six years and another six in the remainder of our first decade. The next few moves required a small trailer behind the Buick, then a small truck, then a very large truck, then a very large house sale plus a very large truck with professional movers.

Church leaders often cannot connect their church activities to church goals.

Along the way we picked up a couple of people named Bob and Kris. Then there were the seemingly endless list of dogs, cats, rats, hamsters, fish, lizards, snakes—you get the picture. Life got a lot more complex. Now we add our parents, who need our help, oh yes, and daughters-in-law, who have pets too. Are you still with me? We have accumulated possessions, people, relationships. We have a history in the work world, and there are many causes competing for our time. At times if you had asked us the purpose of marriage, our answers would have been muddled and confusing. We would have said nice things, but they could have been different things.

Once in a while we would get alone and look into each others eyes and say, "I love you. That is the reason we got married. We didn't get married to work together, to reach

116

the world together. We could have done that alone. We married to be together because that is what we wanted more than anything else." That is what so much of the Marriage Encounter movement and other retreats for couples is about. They revisit the mission, the primal reason for the union.

Marriages struggle and some end when there is not a rekindling of the fire, a regular effort to remind each other of what they said yes to, what they agreed to do.

Churches have the same need, because as time marches on, the church gets more complex, and it accumulates customs and many good activities that hide the primary reason for its existence. Redefinition is the start of a crucial cure for the cluttered church.

A Vague Mission

Often a church has defined itself theologically, but never with respect to mission. Though church dogma is important, few allow it to touch their daily lives with respect to clarifying the mission of their church. You can't redefine what has never been defined—many who quote the Apostles' Creed, say the Lord's Prayer, and sign off on the church's doctrinal statement have very little idea of their church's mission. This is because the leadership think that the vague nature of dogma will excite and mobilize the congregation—"If it gets me excited, then it should excite everyone." To be fair to church leaders, they could simply be so wrapped up in church activity they consider purposeful reflection frivolous.

Thus far we have two reasons to redefine the mission: First, over time the church has accumulated many customs and activities that hide the pristine form of purpose. Second, the church never really did its work; leaders settled for dogma rather than a functional theology of mission that put legs on their mission. Now for a third and very pragmatic reason.

Evaluation

"It's not working. We haven't grown in attendance in some time, in fact we are in a slight decline. Giving is down." This

117

is a normal lament of a pastor or frustrated member at a board meeting or, worse, a church social function that turns ugly. This can be said of at least 80 percent of American congregations, according to the best research.

Attendance and giving are two sure measuring sticks that can reveal problems. Most churches don't do proactive diagnostic probing. They generally wait until something causes corporate pain; then they look for help. When people are leaving a church, saying, "I don't agree with the direction of the church," and leaders don't know enough to respond, the church is in trouble. Often when people don't like the direction of the church, they don't know what they are disagreeing with, because the church doesn't have a defined direction.

Many leaders think because they have a well-crafted purpose statement that they have done their work. This is not enough. There must be a mission statement as well, a statement that defines how their church will engage in the evangelization of the world. The vision for a particular year should state how many people are going to be participating in everything from intentional evangelism to membership in small groups. These vision goals need to be proclaimed from the pulpit, communicated in all printed literature, and done so regularly.

At the end of every year there should be public evaluation of how the church did. The total church effort, the roles of leaders, the money spent, everything should be consistent with the goals for that year, which are built on the church's mission, which is built on the church's purpose, which is built on the church's doctrine. So each church must establish its:

1. Doctrine
2. Purpose
3. Mission
4. Vision/goal
5. Plan
6. Evaluation

This is what will help it stay on course.

The Reformation Journey

I think of reformation as a journey. Not only should we enjoy the journey, we need to recognize its nature. It takes about five years for a church to complete this reformation trip, which involves a growing process that includes frustration, conflict, fatigue, compromise, indecision, lethargy, and worry. The journey map (figure 2) has all these characteristics. While the map may appear like a ride at Disneyland, it was based on our experience with over five hundred congregations and forty-five hundred church leaders during the last seven years. The map was developed, after copious research, by two of T-NET International's training-network team members, Bob Gilliam and Peter Reese. Peter created the concept of the journey and the graphics. Bob created the milestones and subsequent stepping-stones.

It takes about five years for a church to complete this reformation trip.

The map reflects our understanding of how to take a team of church leaders on a 1,000-day journey that brings a church into a new level of fruitfulness. The journey comprises seven milestones, eighteen stepping-stones, and seven major barriers.[1] Many people underestimate the effort, patience, perseverance, and courage required to transform a church. This journey map will help us understand how all of these come into play.

The outline of the work a reformation journey must accomplish is:

I. Redefine your mission
   A. Two milestones
      1. Understand the objective
      2. Analyze the course
II. Redesign your infrastructure
   A. Three milestones
      3. Begin the race

Journey Map

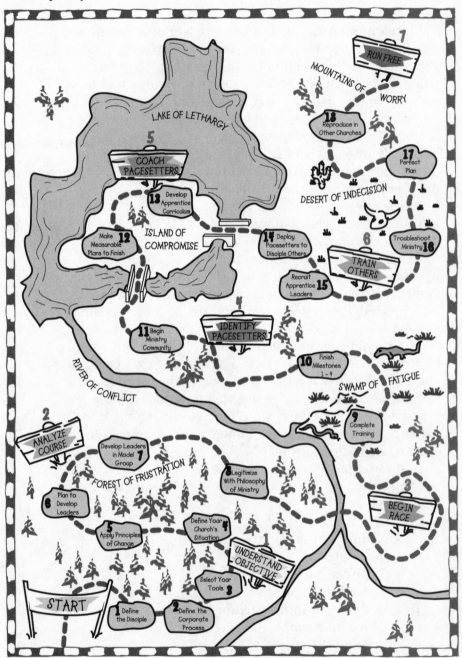

Figure 2

4. Identify pacesetters
5. Coach the pacesetters
III. Reassign our personnel
    A. Two milestones
6. Train others
7. Run free

Milestone 1: Understand the Objective

The first work of art that adorned the wall of our rented apartment was a painting my wife did on a large canvas. It was a copy of the now familiar optical illusion of Jesus. To almost everyone it first looked like an abstract painting. We would invite neighbors in to discuss this profound work. They would stand in front of it and say things like, "It really moves me," "It evokes in me a chaos about the cosmos," or, "Wow," or, "Hmmm." The honest ones would say, "I don't

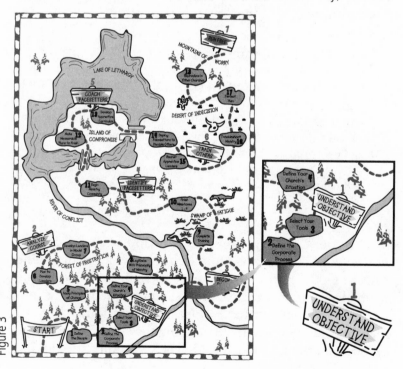

Figure 3

get it." Then we would shock them by explaining that it was a painting of Jesus. Some people never saw it, but the majority who did could see nothing else ever again. The church's objective is much like that: Once you see it, it should never leave your "mind's eye."

One of life's great mysteries is how the church could have missed the obvious goal set for it by God. (At least after it has been explained by a simple and clear exposition of basic biblical texts.) But for many, even after seeing it, they never again refocus their attention on it and its meaning. My only explanation is that this is a devilish scheme to blind the eyes of the church to its basic work. Paul warns us that Satan is full of schemes; he tries to outwit us; he is crafty and tricky (2 Cor. 2:11).

In this day of much corporate prayer, fasting, and reconciliation between denominations and races, the evangelical community agrees on two basic issues that define the goal God has set for the church. They hold strongly to the Great Commandment and the Great Commission.

The Great Commandment

The Great Commandment is found in Matthew's Gospel.

"Love the Lord your God with all your heart and with all your soul and with all your mind." This is the first and greatest commandment. And the second is like it: "Love your neighbor as yourself." All the Law and the Prophets hang on these two commandments.

Matthew 22:37–40

The condensed version is: Love God with everything you've got! This means more than having a warm feeling toward God. Its application is immediately issued in the form of a command to love others, our neighbor being anyone who crosses our path. (Please find authority for this view in Jesus' definition of your neighbor in the story of the Good Samaritan. [Luke 10:25–37].) Whether it is loving

your neighbor, your spouse, your enemies, or other believers, there is only one route to its accomplishment.

The Great Commission

A great commitment to the Great Commission is the only
effective route to the completion of the Great Commandment. The commission is found five times in the New Testament, once in each Gospel and then in the Acts of the
Apostles. If Mark, Luke, John, and Acts are taken together,
you have essentially the command to preach the gospel,
starting in Jerusalem and then gradually to the entire world.
Matthew's version puts "meat on the bones" in that it gives
two primary thrusts.

> Then Jesus came to them and said, "All authority in heaven and
> on earth has been given to me. Therefore go and make disciples
> of all nations, baptizing them in the name of the Father and of the
> Son and of the Holy Spirit, and teaching them to obey everything
> I have commanded you. And surely I am with you always, to the
> very end of the age."
>
> Matthew 28:18–20

The first thrust is to introduce people to Christ and to
baptize them as a sign of their meeting him. This is a one
time event in the life of the Christian. The second thrust is
an ongoing command to teach them "to obey everything I
have commanded you." This means the church is to take
responsibility to train and develop the disciples of the
church, not only in the formative years but for all their
earthly lives.

The Great Commission's imperative is "make disciples"
because they are the only ones who can love God with everything they've got. They are the only ones who want to. Jesus
connected love to obedience in his upper room discourse.
"If you love me, you will obey what I command" (John
14:15). "Whoever has my commands and obeys them, he
is the one who loves me" (John 14:21). "As the Father has

123

loved me, so have I loved you. Now remain in my love. If you obey my commands, you will remain in my love, just as I have obeyed my Father's commands and remain in his love" (John 15:9–10).

From the moment of spiritual birth the Holy Spirit takes up residence in the disciple's spirit. This gives the believer the inclination to obey God and the desire to please God. The disciple proves his or her love for God by stepping out in faith and obeying God's commands. This is a demonstration of a Christian's love for God and neighbors. Christians are to make disciples because only disciples can love; only disciples can bear the fruit that lasts; only disciples can bear much fruit for all of life and so glorify God and prove that they are disciples (John 13:34–35; 15:8, 11–16).

The church's lack of focus or willingness to make the Great Commandment and the Great Commission priority number one is the most grievous corporate sin. It represents the greatest flaw and brings greater shame on the church than anything else because missing God's central calling is the biggest miss of all. While everyone seems to agree that the focus should be these two grand imperatives, there is precious little evidence that we have taken the time to carry them out. Just as with my wife's painting of Jesus, we have seen it, but we have not stayed focused. We have allowed the extraneous, the clutter around us to dilute our effort. We must understand this: *The objective of the church is to intentionally make disciples.*

> *The Great Commission's imperative is "make disciples" because they are the only ones who can love God with everything they've got.*

Stepping-Stones

Stepping-stones are small, incremental accomplishments on the journey. They are crucial because together they get us from milestone to milestone. Being small steps, they are relatively easy to accomplish and provide a sense of progress and, therefore, the needed encouragement to keep moving ahead. For a leadership team to understand the objective, there are three activities or stepping-stones required.

Stepping-Stone 1: Define the Disciple

Earlier I mentioned the disparity between the percentage of pastors versus lay leaders who could identify the purpose of the church. Most pastors could answer the question; most lay leaders could not.

Recently a pastor told me of his experience at a leadership retreat. The church was enrolled in T-NET International's 1,000-day journey, and leaders were given a method to define the disciple. (We give churches a written study with questions that enable them to seek out their own definition of a disciple. Self-discovery is part of defining your

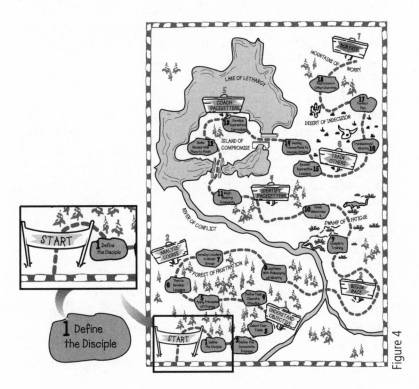

Figure 4

125

primary product as a church. Our ministry is committed to a principled process that insists that churches write their own script.)

The pastor handed out blank pieces of paper to his group of thirty-five and asked this core leadership to define the disciple. He told them, "We are convinced that the focus of the Great Commission, in response to the Great Commandment, is to make disciples." The leaders wrote down their ideas and it was apparent that only three had any real idea. Many of the answers were, "Be like Jesus," or "Love others." The answers were not entirely wrong; they just were not right. They didn't provide enough definition to determine if someone was an obedient disciple or if someone was actually making disciples.

Churches are too much like a shoe factory where everyone agrees to make shoes, but they are turned loose without training and without design specifications to go make their own version of shoes. If you were president of that company and went out onto the manufacturing floor, you would be appalled by what you found, and soon thereafter you'd be out of business.

Because of a simple process that our ministry provided to the church, this pastor was able to work with his leadership to define *disciple*. They were able to answer the Peter Drucker question, "What is your business?" The answer they determined was to glorify God by making disciples. Then they were on their way to answering Drucker's second question, "How is your business?" They could answer, "We have forty-six people in groups or in training to develop the character and ministry skills to become reproducing followers of Christ. We have twenty-four new disciples who are being established in their faith; we have twelve who are in training to take over major leadership roles." They knew *what* they were doing and *how* they were doing.

What a novel idea for any church—that we could actually answer these questions, that we could have more to say than how many bodies were present, how many bucks we took in, and what size building we had! It is not my mission in this book to lay out the process the above church and more than six hundred others have followed. (For more information, contact T-Net International at 800-995-5362.) I will give you one example of the definition of a disciple.

The Cost of Nondiscipleship

Writer Dallas Willard first spoke of the cost of nondiscipleship: the cost to the church and the loss to millions of people is the tragic price the church has paid for its departure from disciple making. This loss includes:

The undedicated hours wasted by millions of semi-obedient Christians.

Thousands of churches of 50 instead of 250.

The ruinous record of intramural fights that have damaged people's faith.

Failure to pass the torch from one spiritual generation to the next.

The diminished lives of pastors who never experience the power of God and the joy of reaching multiplied numbers for Christ.

All these occur because we decided to be generalists, to reduce commitment to the lowest common denominator, to be a clubhouse instead of a lighthouse. Only heaven knows how many lives and how much money has been wasted on what God does not value. Stop paying such a high price for what doesn't count. Start paying the price of what is of greatest value: make disciples. But first figure out what one looks like.

Stepping-Stone 2: Define the Corporate Process

There is no greater issue confronting the local church than its infrastructure. It stands side by side at the head of the priority line with the spiritual revival of the church. In

127

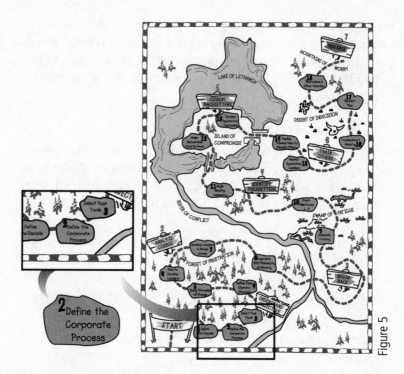

Figure 5

fact the depth and duration of any surge of God's Spirit into the church will be governed by the ability of the church to let God work through the corporate organization. Leaders need to ask, "Do our activities and groups honor our commitment to being faithful and fruitful?"

Once again the best way to surface this need is to get church leaders to engage in a simple exercise. Draw your organizational structure. Our team has many stories, some funny, some sad, of what leaders have drawn. The overall finding is that leaders can't do it or they have very little idea of how a medium-size group of 50 relates to a small group of 10 or to the larger meeting of 150. The following chart gives three examples of the basic infrastructure of a church.

> *There is no greater issue confronting the local church than its infrastructure.*

128

Infrastructure Example: Church of 300

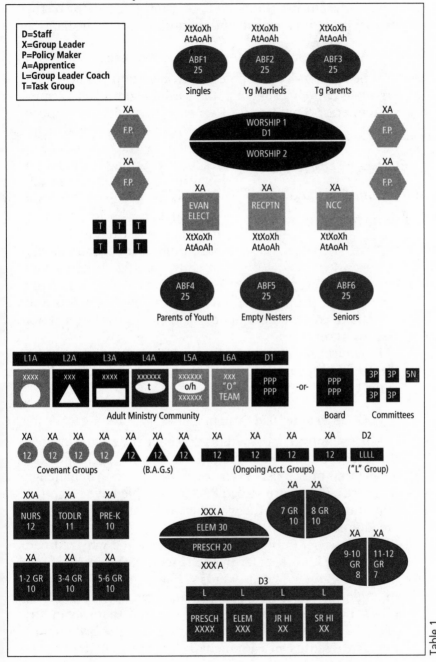

D=Staff
X=Group Leader
P=Policy Maker
A=Apprentice
L=Group Leader Coach
T=Task Group

XtXoXh AtAoAh — ABF1 25 — Singles
XtXoXh AtAoAh — ABF2 25 — Yg Marrieds
XtXoXh AtAoAh — ABF3 25 — Tg Parents

WORSHIP 1 D1 / WORSHIP 2

XA F.P.   XA F.P.   XA F.P.   XA F.P.

XA EVAN ELECT — XtXoXh AtAoAh
XA RECPTN — XtXoXh AtAoAh
XA NCC — XtXoXh AtAoAh

T T T / T T T

ABF4 25 — Parents of Youth
ABF5 25 — Empty Nesters
ABF6 25 — Seniors

L1A xxxx | L2A xxx | L3A xxxx | L4A xxxxxx t | L5A xxxxxx o/h xxxxxx | L6A xxx "O" TEAM | D1 PPP PPP
-or- PPP PPP — Board
3P 3P 5N / 3P 3P — Committees
Adult Ministry Community

XA 12 XA 12 XA 12 XA 12 — Covenant Groups
XA 12 XA 12 XA 12 — (B.A.G.s)
XA 12 XA 12 XA 12 XA 12 — (Ongoing Acct. Groups)
D2 LLLL — ("L" Group)

XXA NURS 12 | XA TODLR 11 | XA PRE-K 10
XA 1-2 GR 10 | XA 3-4 GR 10 | XA 5-6 GR 10

XXX A ELEM 30 / PRESCH 20 XXX A

XA 7 GR 10 | XA 8 GR 10
XA 9-10 GR 8 | XA 11-12 GR 7

D3 — L L L L — PRESCH XXXX | ELEM XXX | JR HI XX | SR HI XX

Table 1

These samples demonstrate that various kinds of groups have different functions. Bob Gilliam, the creator of the charts, provides a legend and definitions for each shape.

Systemic Solutions for Systemic Problems

When pastors feel frustrated and really sharp business leaders avoid church leadership, the reason is not a lack of spiritual interest. The Promise Keepers movement has stripped away that excuse for good, helping men see the importance of leadership. Strong leaders want to be highly committed to a significant work. They don't want to "spin their wheels" attending meetings in a structure with no clear purpose or accountability or consequences. When a successful businessperson attends a church board meeting where most people have not completed assignments and then there are no consequences, the message is, It must not be important.

Almost every effective church understands their system and why they do things the way they do.

I couldn't run a business this way. If these people worked for me, I'd fire them, thinks the businessman. And he is right; it is the church that is wrong.

Good People, Bad System

Most people in poor systems don't like the circumstances. But because they relate the system to some high spiritual karma that only exists in the church, most don't challenge it. These systems are so bad because people have forgotten why things are done the way they are. Usually the reasons are laughable.

On National Public Radio someone asked why railroad tracks were four feet eleven and three-quarter inches from center to center. The answer is: That is the way they were in England, and our system was imported from there. That raises the further question: Why were they that way in England? The answer to that question is that the British railroads carried this measurement over from horse-drawn car-

130

riages. Why were carriages built this way? Apparently the carriage builders used this length because they built the carriages to conform to existing ruts in the road. But how is it possible to have ruts in the road without carriages? Apparently the first ruts came from Roman chariots, when England was toured by conquerors many years before. No one really knows why the Roman chariots had these axle measurements.[2]

Most reasons for setting a system or policy into place make sense at the time. As time passes, however, the history is forgotten and the organization begins to labor over the form-function issues. The functions (like prayer) are scripturally commanded; the forms need to change to help people most effectively work out their salvation.

Good System, Almost Always Good Results

Almost every effective church understands their system and why they do things the way they do. The many studies on the powerful ministries of our time such as the Vineyard, Willow Creek, Calvary Chapels, along with superchurches like Wooddale Community, in Minneapolis, and Saddleback Community, in Mission Viejo, California, all have clear systems that leaders designed, understand, and can explain to others. You point to a single activity and ask, "Why do you hold that meeting with those people twice a month?" They answer with a simple and clear reason.

The interesting thing is that most of the people in the church can answer the question. Redesigning your system may not be the only answer, but it is certainly an indispensable part of the renewal answer.

Dr. Neil Snider, a good friend of mine, is President of Trinity Western University in Langley, British Columbia. The university's motto and purpose is "To train godly Christian leaders." It is Trinity folklore that if you ask anyone on campus the school's purpose, you will get this answer. It has been tested multiple times. People asked a landscape worker what the purpose of TWU was, and he answered, "To train godly Christian leaders."

Good churches, universities, and businesses make sure all members and staff understand their purpose and system.

One of the reason's Rick Warren's baseball diamond (figure 6) has become so popular is that it explains how to develop people with a concept—the baseball diamond—that is understood by virtually all Americans.

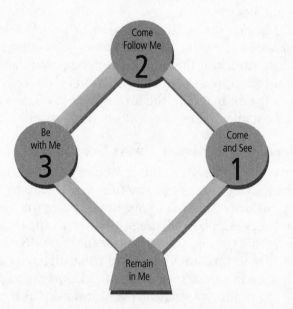

Figure 6

First base = committed to membership of the church
Second base = committed to maturity and growth
Third base = committed to ministry
Home plate = committed to missions[3]

This system, used by Saddleback Community Church, where Warren is the pastor, recognizes that people grow spiritually through stages and that the church should target each stage with relevant ministry. This means the leadership really care about meeting needs and moving people along. It is wonderful stewardship, designed to build the strongest and most fruitful Christians possible. The entire church system is designed to strengthen people and is the backbone of Christian leadership.

My book *New Century Disciple Making* is built around the same principle of process. Jesus' principled approach provides the basis for Warren's updated version.

Rick Warren at Saddleback, Bill Hybels at Willow Creek, and others using many other systems' approaches have recognized the principles Jesus gave us. A good system requires two characteristics: segmentation and sequence.

Segmentation. This simply means that each stage of your system has its own character traits that are designed to meet the needs of people at that stage. The "Come and See" or "First Base" stage would not focus on word studies from the Book of Romans or a theology of missions. While any person should be permitted to get an answer to any serious question, the focus should be, Who is Jesus? and What does it mean to be a Christian? The base ministry unit should be affinity-based small groups that are light in commitment and short in duration and target highly felt needs like parenting and financial health. There will be four types of people at this first-base stage:

Seekers: They are pursuing the purpose and the meaning of life and how Christ might fill the void.

Starters: They are new disciples who need basic grounding in the spiritual journey.

Stagnated: Because of inactivity or neglect, these Christians are not going anywhere. The ministry of the church should address them as well.

Struggling: These Christians have been sidelined by life circumstances; some "acts of God" along with self-inflicted problems are the cause. But they need help in working through the difficult days of their lives.

When you understand your target at each stage, and the specifics of the target group, then you design ministry to address those needs. Since I have written an entire book on the subject, I would refer you to *New Century Disciple Making.*

Sequence. It is common for churches to be strong in one phase of spiritual development and weak in others. There are churches that are great at "Come and See" or "First Base." They attract large groups through the front door, and the draft you feel is the flow from the large front door to the equally large back door from which they are leaving. Usually the problem is that the church has not kept up with the growing needs of new converts. The natural instinct of people is to seek greater learning and challenge. When growing Christians get to a certain level, they want more.

If your church focuses only on introducing people to Christ, you will lose most of those who are growing. Motivated Christians then will seek out a church that provides more spiritual challenge. The problem is not that they want to avoid evangelism. They want to develop as people as well. So people go from one church to another because of the ministry imbalance.

The best type of system is one that moves people from one stage of personal development to the next. In the meantime they are reaching out and being productive because they have become self-aware. They know their gifts and value. This is where the weakness of professional training of potential pastors is most telling. Pastors don't seem to be trained in the most vital of all leadership tasks: understanding and developing people.

A Self-Perpetuating System

A good system creates a multiplication engine that aggressively gathers new people into its community, sorts them out, addresses their needs, and tailors their future. This is not manipulative; it is caring and it takes work. This is why so many leaders want to do it but end up not doing it. They want to do it because it is right and caring. They don't do it because it requires patience and perseverance and it is hard, frustrating work.

I respect Amway and believe it to be an honorable organization. In fact their strategy is very much like what Jesus recommends. I had a very enlightening discussion with one of their most successful leaders. One thing he said really stuck with me: "When most people stop working, their income stops. When I stop working, my income continues." He has built an organization in which he receives residual income because the people he helped build businesses will continue to work even if he doesn't.

I asked him, "Won't they lose motivation and stop working as hard if you don't continue to motivate them?"

He responded that they are already motivated because the most successful members of his team rely on their business for their living. This man makes a very large income and lives an idyllic life of working when he wants. In some respects he serves as an example of what we want in good leaders.

A good church will, like our Amway leader, have highly motivated, well-trained personnel who will work hard and produce regardless of whether or not their leader is there to motivate them. A dynamic church system, then, should not require the constant attention of its leader to keep operating effectively. What any movement requires, as this highly motivating person admitted, is for the leader to regularly do significant acts that keep the vision alive and organizational values paramount.

There is a very big difference between building an Amway distributorship and communicating the gospel; the difference is the tangible versus the intangible. People involved full-time in a marketing business have staked both their purpose and physical needs on its success. The fact that you must make a house payment elevates the daily reality check and thus influences behavior.

The only people who face this kind of reality check in the spiritual realm are clergy. I am not proposing this as a higher virtue, but simply as a reality. Someone who has chosen a professional religious path finds the economics of God's work interwoven into daily life. Ninety-nine percent of

Christians are not required to factor in economics as a motivation to service. The difference is that the church leader must do more motivating and communicating of vision than even the highly motivated businessperson.

There is no greater challenge than to hold the congregation's attention on a consistent basis. I mean holding their attention seven days a week, when they are at work and play. There are so many distractions, so many varieties of good things and causes into which they can pour money and energy. So it is imperative for leaders to build self-perpetuating systems that provide intrinsic motivation and rewards. But the leader must be vigilant to communicate vision and keep the system's main working parts oiled so that they drive the results.

Stepping-Stone 3: Select Your Tools

When we bought our first home I asked a seasoned homeowner to accompany me to Sears to purchase my first set of gardening tools. I grew up in an apartment, spent college in the athletic dorm, then joined my bride in another apartment. After eight years of marriage and two sons, we purchased our first home. As you might guess, I was without portfolio with regard to a husband's calling to "yard work." I walked the aisles and was immediately drawn to the electric power tools, but my friend convinced me to save money and get all muscle-driven stuff.

> *There is no greater challenge than to hold the congregation's attention on a consistent basis.*

This ill-fated decision led to needless hours, turning chores into sweaty crusades. It led to sore backs, evening plans canceled because of fatigue, and unfinished work. Later I found out from others that my "tool time" counselor borrowed power tools from neighbors. He was just cheap!

Twenty-one years later I look out my window and admire my gravel yard, my cement patio, the foliage that the gardener cuts, and the flowers that Jane plants, waters, pulls dead out of the ground, and replants. It's a wonderful life. I learned something from my experience: Select both your tools and tool counselors very carefully.

It's Tool Time

Once you understand your objective, you have defined your product, and you have outlined the design for your disciple-making system, you want tools that will assist you in achieving what you desire to accomplish. Far too many churches simply look for the "hottest" or best-looking materials that everybody uses. Churches put about as much study into small-group materials as many men do into their wardrobes—not much. I know many men who allow their wife to buy their clothes (what barbarians!). My wife isn't allowed to buy my clothes, only to wear them around the house after she has shrunk them in the wash.

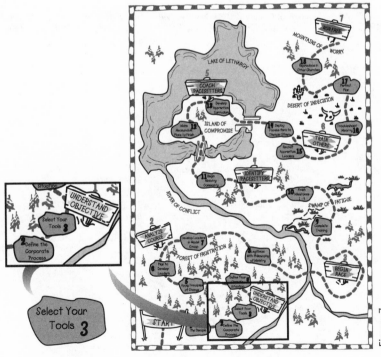

Figure 7

137

Churches must select materials, or tools, that meet the needs of their members. The tools they select should be governed by their objective. The steps are simple:

1. Identify your objective for the group or individual. (A good criterion is to make sure your group scores a "bull's-eye" on your church's mission statement.)
2. Make sure your objective fits the larger church goal and priority of order of starting new ministries.
3. Research available materials for each phase of spiritual development (Warren's Baseball Diamond or any other phased concepts that you have developed or adapted). I have included two examples of how this works. The first looks at general materials; the second shows what we did with the Southern Baptist Sunday School Board.

Comparison of Different Disciple-Making Approaches

Group NAVS (CDM)	Come and See (MODERATE)	Come Follow Me (STRONG)	Be with Me (STRONG)	Remain in Me (MODERATE)
	*Jesus Cares for Women *One-on-One *Eclectic	*2:7, Bks 1–2	*2:7, Bks 3–5	*Eclectic
CHURCHES ALIVE	(STRONG) *One-on-One *Assurance *Discovery Class	(STRONG) *Design for Discipleship *Love One Another *God-in-You	(WEAK)	(WEAK)
CHURCH DYNAMICS	(STRONG) *One-on-One *Guest Follow-up *New Christian Follow-up	(SHALLOW) *Basic Discipleship *Basic Evangelism	(SHALLOW) *Process II *Process III *(Very few involved in 2:7)	(NONE)
SERENDIPITY	(MATERIALS ONLY) *101 Level *201 Lifestyle *Support Groups *301 Book Studies	(MATERIALS ONLY) *301 Book Studies *401 Book/Topic Studies	(MATERIALS ONLY) None	(MATERIALS ONLY) *301 Book Studies *401 Book/Topic Studies
EQUIPPING THE SAINTS	NONE	(STRONG) *Book 1 *Book 2	(STRONG) *Book 3	(STRONG) *Book 4
WILLOW CREEK	(STRONG) Walking w/God I	(STRONG) Walking w/God II		
BROADMAN PRESS	(STRONG) Survival Kit Support Groups	(STRONG) MasterLife	(STRONG) MasterBuilder Experiencing God	(STRONG) Many Materials

Table 2

Come and See Phase

Product Description
1. Has made a decision to trust Christ as Savior.
2. Has assurance of salvation.
3. Understands need for Bible study, prayer, fellowship.
4. Understands the purpose of a church and his or her need for it.
5. Understands God's will for him or her to be a disciple and what is involved.
6. Has tasted the relevance of ministry.
7. Has a vision for what he or she could become/do.
8. Has seen discipleship modeled.
9. Has seen the gospel shared.
10. Has been challenged to share your vision and become a disciple.
11. Has been given time to make a solid decision.

Environment
1. Learn who Jesus Christ is.
2. Learn how his Word fits into his life.
3. Hear someone model simple communication with God in prayer.
4. Understand how brothers and sisters in the faith fellowship in the church and why.
5. Clearly appreciate their unbelieving friends, right where they are, still outside of Christ, and begin to love them toward the Savior.
6. Experience whatever healing is necessary in a positive setting.
7. See new life in Christ as a total change in the eyes of God.
8. Be exposed to excellent models of disciples.

Possible Curriculum Options

	Produce Product	My Role	Educ Level	Commit Level	Proper Phase	Process Included	Church Orient
Navs Lessons on Assurance	P	O	Jr. Hi	L	Y	N	Y
Navs Growing in Christ (inc. LOA)	Y	O	Jr. Hi	M	Y	Y	Y
C.A. Discovery Class	Y	O	Jr. Hi	L	Y	Y	Y
C.A. Are You My Friends	P	O	Jr. Hi	L	Y	N	Y
C.A. God's Family	P	O	Jr. Hi	L	Y	N	Y
Serendipity 101	P	C, A	H.S.	A	Y	N	Y
Serendipity 201	P	C, A	H.S.	A	Y	N	Y
Serendipity Support Groups	P	C, A	H.S.	L	Y	N	Y
Serendipity 301 Book Studies	P	C, A	H.S.	A	Y	N	Y
B.P. Survival Kit for New Christians 1	y	O	Jr. Hi	M	Y/N	P	Y
B.P. Conquering Chemical Dependency	P	A	H.S.	H	Y/N	Y	Y
B.P. Conquering Eating Disorders	P	A	H.S.	H	Y/N	Y	Y
B.P. Conquering Codependency	P	A	H.S.	H	Y/N	Y	Y
B.P. Hurtful Family Experiences	P	A	H.S.	H	Y/N	Y	Y
B.P. Search for Significance	P	A	H.S.	H	Y/N	Y	Y
B.P. A Time for Healing	P	A	H.S.	H	Y/N	Y	Y
CCC Ten Basic Steps (1–3)	Y	A	Jr. Hi	M	Y	Y	Y
W.C. Walking with God I	Y	A	H.S.	M	Y	Y	Y

Produce Product	Y = Yes	P = Partially	N = No	
My Role	C = Creator	A = Adapter	O = Adopter	
Commitment Level	L = Low	M = Medium	H = High	A = All

Table 3

139

Come Follow Me Phase

Product Description
1. Has a vision to reach others for Christ.
2. Seeks to learn even when lessons are difficult.
3. Disciplined to keep spiritual priorities on top.
4. Committed to give up home/possessions/family.
5. Modeling after Christ.
6. Strong enough to withstand opposition/hunger/hatred.
7. Involved in a small accountability group with a good model for over six months.
8. Established in the fundamentals—Bible study, prayer, fellowship, witnessing.
9. Ready to train others in these basics.

Environment
1. A leader who is a coach.
2. Firm accountability.
3. Accountability practiced in love.
4. Focus on building habits.

Possible Curriculum Options

	Produce Product	My Role	Educ Level	Commit Level	Proper Phase	Process Included	Church Orient
Navs Growing Strong	Y	O	Coll.	M	Y	Y	Y
Navs 2:7, Books 1 and 2	Y	O	Coll.	M	Y	Y	Y
Navs DFD, Books 1–3	Y	O	H.S.	L/M	Y	Y	Y
C.A. Love One Another	Y	A, O	H.S.	L/M	Y	Y/N	Y
C.A. God in You	Y	A, O	H.S.	L/M	Y	Y/N	Y
C.D.I. One-to-One Discipleship	P	O	H.S.	L/M	Y	Y	Y
C.D.I. One-on-One Evangelism	P	O	H.S.	M	Y	N	Y
Serendipity 301 Book Studies	P	C, A	H.S	A	Y	N	Y
Serendipity 401 Topic Studies	P	C, A	H.S.	A	Y	N	Y
E.T.S. Books 1 and 2	Y	O	Coll.	H	Y	Y	Y
B.P. Survival Kit for New Christians 1, 2	Y	O	Jr. Hi	L	Y	P	Y
B.P. Survival Kit for New Christians 3	P	O	H.S.	L	Y	P	Y
B.P. The Doctrine of Prayer	P	A	H.S.	A	Y	Y	Y/SS
B.P. MasterLife I	Y	O	H.S.	M	Y	N	Y
B.P. MasterLife II	Y	O	H.S.	M	Y	N	Y
B.P. Step by Step Through the OT	P	A	H.S.	A	2/3/4	Y	Y
B.P. Step by Step Through the NT	P	A	H.S.	A	2/3/4	Y	Y
B.P. Partners with God	P	A	H.S.	A	2/3	Y	Y
W.C. Walking with God II	Y	A	H.S.	L/M	Y	Y	Y
CCC Ten Basic Steps (4–10)	Y	A	H.S.	M	Y	Y	Y

Produce Product	Y = Yes	P = Partially	N = No
My Role	C = Creator	A = Adapter	O = Adopter SS = Sun. School
Commitment Level	L = Low	M = Medium	H = High A = All

Table 4

140

Be with Me Phase

Product Description

1. Has about two years of relevant ministry experience.
2. Modeling Jesus' ministry.
3. Boldly declaring God's truth to a pagan world.
4. Maturely handling rejection.
5. Compassion for the lost.
6. Willing to suffer/lose all/die for Christ.
7. Abiding in God's Word.
8. Deep love for Christians.
9. Modeling servant leadership.
10. Depending on God to meet needs.
11. Bearing fruit.
12. Making disciples who make disciples.
13. Leading and training others.

Environment

1. A group meeting that oozes with vision for the church.
2. Leaders that encourage initiative and discourage turfguarding.
3. A place where individual and team accomplishments are acknowledged and celebrated regularly.
4. A place that facilitates bidirectional communication between leaders and disciples.
5. A place that provides continual training and growth in ministry skills.
6. A place that always provides nurture.
7. A place that continues to provide loving accountability.
8. A place that never lets leaders forget the basics.
9. A place that perpetuates the delegation of ministry to trained apprentices.

Possible Curriculum Options

	Produce Product	My Role	Educ Level	Commit Level	Proper Phase	Process Included	Church Orient
Navs 2:7, Books 3 through 5	Y	O	Coll.	H	Y	Y	P
Navs Thinking through Discipleship	Y	A	H.S.	M/H	Y	N	Y
Discipleship	Y	A	H.S.	M/H	Y	N	Y
Navs DFD, Books 5–7	P	O	H.S.	M	?	Y	Y
C.D.I. Process II	?	O	H.S.	M	Y	Y	Y
C.D.I. Process III	?	O	H.S.	M	Y	Y	Y
E.T.S. Books 3–4	Y	A	Coll.	H	Y	Y	P
B.P. Master Your Money	P	A/O	H.S.	A	3/4	Y	Y
B.P. MasterBuilder	Y/Ldr	O	H.S.	M	3	Y	Y
B.P. Disciple's Prayer Life	P	A/O	H.S.	M	3/4	Y	Y
B.P. MasterDesign	P	A/O	H.S.	A	3/4	Y	Y
B.P. Experiencing God	P	A	H.S.	A	3/4	Y	Y
B.P. Step by Step Through the OT	P	A	H.S.	A	2/3/4	Y	Y
B.P. Step by Step Through the NT	P	A	H.S.	A	2/3/4	Y	Y
B.P. Partners with God	P	A	H.S.	A	2/3	Y	Y
B.P. The Mind of Christ	P	A	H.S.	A	3/4	Y	Y
B.P. Fresh Encounter	P	A	H.S.	A.	3/4	Y	Y

Produce Product   Y = Yes   P = Partially   N = No

My Role   C = Creator   A = Adapter   O = Adopter

Commitment Level   L = Low   M = Medium   H = High   A = All

Table 5

141

Remain in Me Phase

Product Description
1. Constant growth in character and fruitfulness.

Environment
1. An experience in which individuals are continually nurtured and challenged to continue their spiritual growth.
2. An experience in which participants are held lovingly accountable to continue to apply the basics as well as to grow in obedience.
3. An experience that allows participants to focus more on life-oriented problems than on a preconceived curriculum.
4. An experience that develops a community out of the participants and enables them to minister to and with one another.
5. An experience of growth and love that lasts a lifetime.

Possible Curriculum Options

	Produce Product	My Role	Educ Level	Commit Level	Proper Phase	Process Included	Church Orient
Navs Life Change Series	Y	A	Coll.	H	Y	N	Y
Navs Thinking through Discipleship	Y	A	H.S.	M/H	Y	N	Y
Serendipity 301 Book Studies	Y	C, A	H.S.	M/H	Y	N	Y
Serendipity 401 Topic Studies	Y	C, A	H.S.	M/H	Y	N	Y
E.T.S. Book 4	Y	A	Coll.	H	Y	Y	Y
B.P. The Biblical Basis of Missions	P	A	H.S.	A	Y	Y	Y
B.P. Disciple's Prayer Life	P	A/O	H.S.	M	3/4	Y	Y
B.P. MasterDesign	P	A/O	H.S.	A	3/4	Y	Y
B.P. Experiencing God	Y	A	H.S.	A	3/4	Y	Y
B.P. Step by Step Through the OT	P	A	H.S.	A	2/3/4	Y	Y
B.P. Step by Step Through the NT	P	A	H.S.	A	2/3/4	Y	Y
B.P. The Mind of Christ	P	A	H.S.	A	3/4	Y	Y
B.P. Fresh Encounter	P	A	H.S.	A	3/4	Y	Y
The Bible	Y	C, A	All	A	Y	N	Y
Various Topics	Y	C	A	A	Y	N	Y
Christian Books	Y	C	A	A	Y	N	Y

Produce Product	Y = Yes	P = Partially	N = No
My Role	C = Creator	A = Adapter	O = Adopter
Commitment Level	L = Low	M = Medium	H = High	A = All

Table 6

142

Generic Model of the Disciple
at the End of Each Phase of Discipleship

Phase/Timing/ Major Focus	Characteristics/Skills at End of Each Phase Successive phases assume the characteristics of prior phases continue.
Come and See (6–12 months) Attraction and Evangelism	1. Has made a decision to trust Christ as Savior (John 1:49). 2. Has assurance of salvation (John 1:50–51). 3. Understands the *need* for worship, Bible study, prayer, and fellowship (Mark 1:14–18). 4. Understands the purpose of the church and his/her need for it. 5. Understands God's will for him/her to be a disciple and what is involved (John 4:34–38). 6. Has observed ministry that is relevant and is developing a taste for it (John 4:2). 7. Is developing God's vision for his/her character and ministry involvement (John 4:34–38). 8. Has seen the initial process of discipleship modeled (John 4:42). 9. Has seen the gospel shared with another person (John 4:40–41). 10. Has been challenged to become an accountable disciple (a person who grows in keeping his/her commitments to God in the context of loving relationships) and has been given time to make a solid decision about the challenge (John 4:35). 11. Has publicly identified with Christ through baptism (John 4:2).
Come Follow Me (9–12 months) Establishing Basic Christian Habits	1. Has learned to be *intentional* in the ministry he/she chooses to do (Mark 1:38). 2. Has learned the importance of submission to God and desires to submit (Luke 5:5). 3. Is beginning to recognize God at work (Luke 5:8). 4. Is learning the importance of developing *godly inner character* over the mere external observances of God's commands (Matt. 12:1–8). 5. Is habitual in the spiritual fundamentals (worship, Bible study, Scripture memory, prayer, fellowship, evangelism, and stewardship of time, talents, and money) (Matt. 6:52; 13:23). 6. Has a vision to be instrumental in reaching others for Christ (Matt. 9:37–38). 7. Spends social time with unbelievers who need exposure to believers (Mark 2:15–17). 8. Seeks to learn—even when lessons are difficult (Matt. 13:10–11). 9. Is committed to love and serve Christ before family, home, and possessions (Matt. 8:19–22). 10. Is modeling his/her life after Christ (Luke 6:40). 11. Is, by the Spirit's enablement, able to withstand hardship and opposition (Luke 6:20–26). 12. Is involved in a small accountability group with a good model for over 6 months (all passages). 13. Is ready to train others in these basic habits (Matt. 10:1–11:1). 14. Can identify and is using his/her spiritual giftedness in ministry. 15. Is regularly observing the Lord's Supper.
Be with Me (2 years) Training and Deployment in Leading Ministries	1. Has completed about 2 years of relevant ministry (all passages). 2. Is modeling Jesus' ministry (Matt. 10:25). 3. Is boldly declaring God's truth to a lost (pagan) world (Matt. 10:5–7). 4. Maturely handles rejection (Matt. 10:14). 5. Has a love/compassion for saved and unsaved compelling him/her to meet needs (Matt. 9:36–38). 6. Is willing to suffer, to lose all, or even to die for Christ (Luke 14:26). 7. Continuing to practice basic Christian habits while adding new ones (Luke 9:10). 8. Is able to discern between man's version of God's teaching and God's intent behind his Word (Matt. 5:21–48). 9. Is willing to lovingly confront sin in the life of another believer (Matt. 18:15).

(Continued)

Table 7

143

Phase/Timing/ Major Focus	Characteristics/Skills at End of Each Phase Successive phases assume the characteristics of prior phases continue.
	10. Models servant leadership or servant followership according to giftedness (John 13). 11. Depends upon God to meet needs (Matt. 10:5–10). 12. Is bearing fruit (developing godly character and leading others to Christ) (John 15:8). 13. Is making disciples who themselves make disciples (Matt. 28:19–20). 14. Is regularly contributing from his/her financial resources to the ministry (Matt. 6:2).
Remain in Me (the rest of your life) Multiplying Disciple Makers	1. Continues to grow in godly character (John 16:16; Col. 1:28). 2. Continues to reproduce self in others (2 Tim. 2:2). 3. Continues involvement in ministry (John 15:8; Rom. 12:6). 4. Continues to share Christ (Matt. 28:19). 5. Is often sent into the world as God's minister or servant (Acts 1:8).

Table 7 continued

The other procedures are on building people through proper selection of tools and these will be addressed under Milestone 3, Stepping-Stone 7—Develop Leaders in Model Group.

The Major Barrier: Lack of Understanding

Each milestone has a major barrier. For Milestone 1 it is *actually understanding the objective*. Briefly allow me to mention a few reasons why grasping the focus of reforming around the disciple-making imperative is so challenging.

Language

Words mean something, and the way we use them reveals our worldview. When people use the expression "evangelism and discipleship," they generally mean telling people about Christ and then training new Christians. The language implies separation in the two processes where none is needed. This leads to an unintentional miniaturization of the Great Commission.

To be fair, *discipleship* usually means working with those who are already Christians, especially newly converted Christians. I would consider *discipleship* a term relevant to all of a disciple's life journey. *Disciple making,* however, refers to evangelism, outreach of every kind, training and nurturing of any kind, and local and cross-cultural missions of any kind. The danger of misusing the words is to misuse the church and to abuse the called ministers who are to be prepared for the disciple-making task. It also makes disciple making just one of the many good activities of the congregation. It leads away from a proper focus on a transformed person called a disciple. It militates against the objective proposed in this work.

Pastoral Expectations

A pastor is forced to deal with expectations that come from three sources: what the pastor expects from himself, what the church expects, and what the clerical community thinks. When a leader is young, all of these burn bright and influence most of his actions. He eventually comes to terms with what he expects from himself. He accepts who he is and what he does well and not so well. Otherwise a serious pathology of deep insecurity develops, which means that he will seek acceptance in various ways from the abovementioned groups that usually are abusive to the pastor, his family, and the church. This insecurity sidetracks the pastor, so that he can't be productive.

While the first and usually most unaccepting force is oneself, the second most difficult is the congregation. Pastors must live with their congregation. Congregants expect pastors to live up to a certain kind of image that fulfills a (usually dated) paradigm of leadership. This struggle always goes on, and until acceptance or a truce is found, the battle rages.

I followed as pastor a greatly loved man thirty years my senior in a traditional church setting. He worked eighty hours a week and visited people in their homes and at the hospital. He was always present at all church social events and spent very little time preparing sermons or developing leadership. Additionally he was gifted in communicating love, in fact he hugged every parishioner departing worship.

I am not gifted at communicating warmth. I am six feet six inches tall and hard to hug. I didn't visit people in their homes. I spent a lot of time in sermon preparation and in training leaders. My focus was to build a few good leaders who in turn would multiply their impact through others. This was interpreted as not loving people, not caring about their lives, and generally being selfish. The fact is I spent a good share of my time doing the very same things as my predecessor, but his image was burned into their memories. That was what a pastor was like.

If we want to lead churches to be multiplying Great Commandment and Great Commission churches, we need to settle the acceptance questions.

It took me several years to prove myself to the majority of the people and to convince them there was more than one way to pastor a church. During this difficult and very painful time, I was told more than once that if I would just back off the Great Commission—the Christian's call to share the faith—my life would be easier. The move from an antiquated pastoral and church paradigm to one that focused on the Great Commandment and the Great Commission caused the struggle because the church didn't understand the objective.

The desire to be accepted by fellow pastors goes away the quickest, but still is very powerful in the first decade of ministry. We must come to the place where we know what we are doing is the best for our church, regardless of what other ministers may say. A healthy balance is to care about what colleagues think of our integrity, for example, but not so much of what they think of our preaching style. If we want to lead churches to be multiplying Great Commandment and Great Commission churches, we need to settle the acceptance questions.

No One Seems to Get It

The fact that pastors don't get out of their difficult position must be filed under *mystery*. I have often lamented, wondered, and prayed about why grasping the obvious directives of the Great Commandment and Great Commission has been so difficult for the church. We have made small what God meant to be big. We have made complex what is simple. We have made the obvious a mystery. I am sure it is a combination of culture, the flesh, and the sinister strategy of the evil one. The enemy plots to get us to dilute our purpose, to dedicate ourselves to the good instead of the best.

Lord, remove the scales from our eyes.

Milestone 2: Analyze the Course

Your church leaders are committed to the reformation journey. You know your objective; you know your product; you have a process; you have selected your tools; now what? It would be prudent to look at the journey ahead and develop a strategy for the trip.

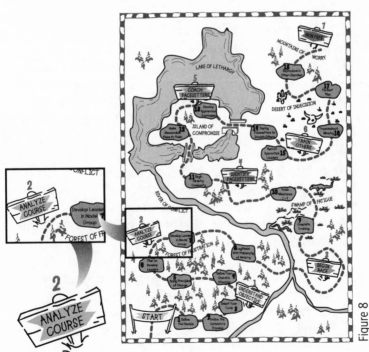

Figure 8

My youngest son is creative, thoughtful, godly, and twenty-four. He plans many things well, including all the important things. He is also somewhat of a daredevil: Bungee jumping, rock climbing, shopping with his mother are all "run of the mill" for Kris. Recently he combined his propensity for bungee jumping and daredevilry when he said, "Hey, Dad, I want to go to New York City for a computer show. Can you get me a frequent flier ticket?" I am very popular because of these tickets.

"Why are you going?" I quizzed.

"Curt and I are going to look for jobs." (Curt lives in Minneapolis; we live in San Diego.)

"Tell me your plan." That was good! I learned this technique through many years of trial and error. This is better than, "Are you nuts?"

"Well," Kris sighed. "Curt and I will meet at the airport in New York."

"So where are you staying and how do you plan to get to the computer show and where is it?"

"We thought we could just sleep in the airport, then take a taxi to the show, stay for a few hours, then fly home."

"So what do you think you would feel like and look like as you went to your job interviews?" I sat back and waited. It was obvious that Kris and Curt's great adventure needed some more thought. Oh, by the way, when your son is a man, you don't tell him he *can't* go. You bring up "stuff" as a reality check. The two young men were completely capable of making the trip a success but they needed to be reminded to analyze the course. The trip was canceled because it turned out there was a better deal in San Francisco.

The first phase of a successful journey is good planning. If one is driving across the United States, the operative questions are, "What route will we take?" "How long will it take?" "What will it cost?" "Where will we stop and rest?" and "What is the condition of our vehicle?"

The answers to these questions will also govern the quality and success of the reformation journey. The team at T-NET International has had experience as fellow travelers in this very journey with more than seven hundred congregations. This has yielded the following answers.

What Route Should We Take?

To determine the best route, we must map out the direction we want to go. Should we take the northern route or the southern route? There is snow and ice on the northern route in winter and the desert is 120 degrees in the summer on the southern route, so we must use common sense.

A leadership team wants to take the most direct route and one that fits the time they have and one they have the capacity to handle. Leaders must know their objective, since every church goes at a different speed over a different route. Some have more barriers and fewer personnel. Some common, unavoidable barriers must be crossed, but each church can do so in its own way.

> *How long the transformation lasts depends on how long the church continues to practice the new habits they have acquired.*

How Long Will It Take?

Most churches require five years of steady determination to transform the congregation in a lasting way. Short-term change in churches abounds. However, just as precious stones take longer to create, so does true reformation.

T-NET International formally works with churches for 1,000 days, and about 50 percent of the churches experience profound turnarounds in that time frame. Another 30 percent do so at the end of four to five years, while 20 percent don't experience true reformation at all. Most of the latter are due to pastoral changes and conflict on issues unrelated to the training. Some, though, just don't respond to our training.

How long the transformation lasts depends on how long the church continues to practice the new habits they have acquired. It is very much like getting a group of people into good physical condition. How long they stay in shape depends entirely on how long they continue to exercise.

How Much Will It Cost?

Churches always think training costs too much. They are afflicted with a strange myopia that says, It is smart to spend 2.5 million dollars on a building but it is outrageous to spend five thousand dollars a year improving on what we actually do. No one in his or her right mind would say, "Let's spend millions on a future ash heap and nothing on what lasts forever." No, we don't say that, we just go and do it. The church isn't called to be a building contractor; it is called to build people, develop leaders, make disciples, and evangelize the world. Somewhere the church got the idea that spiritual things are free, and what really costs money are parking lots, pews, and hymnals.

The reformation journey is not a sprint but a long-distance expedition.

Reformation will not cost the church much money. The high price of reformation is time and effort. When you consider the cost of discipleship, be aware that it will cost your most precious nonretrievable commodity: time.

Reformation leaders also will pay the price with emotional energy. It will mean being criticized unfairly by those threatened by change. It will require some lifestyle changes, missing that fishing trip, golf match, or playoff game because of a scheduling conflict. Just remember, the cost of not doing it is much higher; it is called a wasted life.

Where Will We Stop and Rest?

The reformation journey is not a sprint but a long-distance expedition. While marathon runners don't plan to stop, they have stations where they take on more fluid and various forms of new energy. Our journey is much longer than a marathon and will require many stops for rest and rejuvenation.

150

You may recall the television series *Wagon Train*. Every week the wagon train, led by Ward Bond, would make a little progress but they would always encounter trouble of some kind. The story centered on the drama of solving the problem. The strange thing about *Wagon Train* is that the series was canceled before they got anywhere.

It might be wise to think of the reformation journey as more like *Wagon Train* than modern flight, speed trains, or even automobiles. The pioneers stopped and rested a lot. Often the drama described how they made the wrong turn, encountered a storm, or had a group that wanted to turn back. It is vital for a church team to pace itself, to take time out to renew the vision, to heal wounds, to reaffirm commitments.

Stepping-Stones

There are three stepping-stones that lead to reaching the second milestone. They are: Define your church's situation, know the principles of change, and have a plan for developing leaders. When we ask, What is the condition of our vehicle? the answer leads us to the next stepping-stone.

Stepping-Stone 4: Define Your Church's Situation

What do we have to work with? What are our resources? What kind of spiritual condition are we in? These questions must be answered honestly by church leaders. Unless we are willing to face our own reality, there is no chance of reformation.

There are a number of ways to come to the point of repentance. This may mean that a person will have to say, "I have been wrong morally." For a church it means confessing, "We have been wrong in our methods (or in our objectives)." This wrongness could simply stem from a lack of definition, neglect, or ignorance. It very often simply means being locked in a paradigm that once was effective but now

151

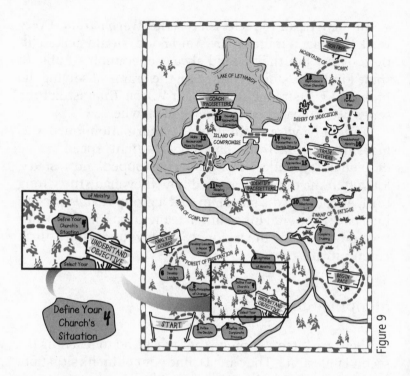

Figure 9

is the greatest barrier to growth. For example, a Sunday evening service that was designed to reach people may have become a negative experience that people want to fight about. It's the classic two-bald-men-fighting-over-a-hairbrush syndrome.

The easy things to identify are condition of finances and attendance figures. Understanding why these obvious health gauges decline is the real challenge. To identify the causes, go back to your infrastructure issues of why each type of group exists and what each one's mission is. For example, Sunday evening services usually decline because they simply repeat the Sunday morning worship. It is the same "sit and listen" experience, except the sermon is not as good, the crowd is smaller, and the choir isn't there. It's a downer.

We may come to repentance on these issues because our "gut reaction" says something isn't right here. Through prayer on both an individual and corporate level, God cre-

152

ates in the leaders a clear sense of dissatisfaction. They make a commitment: We can do better. We pledge to do better.

Hard Data

The hard data approach is not less spiritual but it addresses the mind more than the spirit. It helps us understand our condition. When I go to the doctor because I feel pain, I want to know his diagnosis. My personal physician is very detailed. He draws pictures and makes notes for his patients. I always return home with notes, diagrams, and a prescription. I wouldn't like it if he patted me on the back and said, "Bill, I know it hurts, I will pray for you."

The diagnostic tool we employ is the Spiritual Journey Evaluation. This asks a series of questions that reveal a congregation's spiritual health. I have provided a few of our questions that deal with everything from larger strategic issues to how many people are reading the Bible or sharing their faith.

I have also included the results from one of our training centers, What Impact Looks Like. From this survey, a church can determine exactly what needs to be worked on.

Earlier I covered the four disciple-making phases modeled by Christ. Figure 6 showed the baseball-diamond example from Saddleback Community Church. The Spiritual Journey Evaluation measures where your congregation is with regard to the phases. Most churches cannot sustain reformation because they really don't understand their own church. So this step involves defining your church's situation. Part of doing that is discovering where your people are and what they need to develop. Once you have accurate information, you can design priorities for your journey. This evaluation tells you how many groups you will need at each level of spiritual development.

Most churches interested in growth either find a megachurch program they like or read about a program they'd like to duplicate. They "roll the dice," hoping that this will work for them as well.

Spiritual Journey Evaluation

It is certainly true that the experience of spiritual growth and discipleship is a process. This process takes time, involves many steps, and for most is somewhat erratic, including stops along the way to catch one's breath. The Bible tells us that the Good Shepherd knows his sheep. Additionally, Peter writes that church leaders are to "shepherd the flock of God." To do our job and help you along your spiritual journey, we must know our sheep just like Jesus does. To enable us to do this, would you please thoughtfully complete the following checklist. Thank you for helping us to be the best shepherds we can be.

For questions 1–26, please use the following scale:
1 = strongly disagree   2 = somewhat disagree   3 = somewhat agree   4 = strongly agree
Please circle your answer.

1. I have finalized my decision to trust Christ as Savior. — 1 2 3 4
2. I am absolutely sure I'll go to heaven when I die. — 1 2 3 4
3. I understand the need for personal Bible study, prayer, fellowship, and sharing my faith. — 1 2 3 4
4. I understand the purpose of the church and my need for it. — 1 2 3 4
5. I understand that it is God's will for me to be a growing disciple and what is involved in this. — 1 2 3 4
6. I have experienced the relevance of ministry. — 1 2 3 4
7. I have a clear picture of what God generally wants me to do in ministering to others. — 1 2 3 4
8. I have seen discipleship modeled and have been challenged to grow as a disciple. — 1 2 3 4
9. I have seen the gospel shared effectively. — 1 2 3 4
10. I am committed enough to join a weekly small group (not just Sunday school) or one-on-one relationship that will hold me lovingly accountable to turn the beliefs listed in question 3 above into life habits. — 1 2 3 4
11. I feel an internal desire to minister to and reach others for Christ. — 1 2 3 4
12. I am consciously trying to model my life after Christ, not just mentally but behaviorally. — 1 2 3 4
13. I am usually willing to suffer rather than yield to temptation. — 1 2 3 4
14. I am consistently involved in some ministry, at least as an apprentice. — 1 2 3 4
15. I am presently involved in a small group or one-on-one relationship with (a) mature Christian leader(s), which will last at least nine months, in which I am finally developing consistent habits of daily devotions, frequent Bible study, prayer, evangelism, and Christian priorities. — 1 2 3 4
16. At one time I developed some or all of the habits described in question 15 above, but I maintained those habits for less than one year. — 1 2 3 4
17. I have completed the challenge of consistently practicing the habits of daily devotions, frequent Bible study, prayer, and evangelism for a period of at least one year. — 1 2 3 4
18. I am consistently involved in a ministry and could train an apprentice to do what I do. — 1 2 3 4
19. I am bearing fruit. — 1 2 3 4
20. I can maturely handle temptation, suffering, and rejection most of the time. — 1 2 3 4
21. I am presently continuing to consistently practice the habits of daily devotions, frequent Bible study, and prayer. — 1 2 3 4
22. I am presently continuing to consistently practice the habit of sharing the gospel with unbelievers. — 1 2 3 4
23. I am involved in a relationship, small group, or leader training where I am consistently held accountable to practice the basics and grow beyond them, or I am willing to become involved in such a relationship or group. — 1 2 3 4
24. I am training others to do what I do in ministry or to do another ministry. — 1 2 3 4
25. I am constantly abiding in Christ and my behavior is actually continuing to change to be like him. — 1 2 3 4
26. I have been training apprentices or equipping others for ministry for more than two years and would continue to do so even if no one supervised me. — 1 2 3 4

(Continued)

For questions 27–31, please use the following scale:

1 = almost every day   6 = about once a month
2 = 3 to 5 times a week   7 = about once a quarter
3 = several times a week   8 = about once a year
4 = about once a week   9 = less than once a year
5 = several times a month 10 = never

27. How often do you have a personal time of Bible reading and prayer?   1 2 3 4 5 6 7 8 9 10
28. How often do you study your Bible?   1 2 3 4 5 6 7 8 9 10
29. How often do you pray for more than five minutes?   1 2 3 4 5 6 7 8 9 10
30. How often do you share the gospel?   1 2 3 4 5 6 7 8 9 10
31. How often do you lead a person to receive Christ as Savior?   1 2 3 4 5 6 7 8 9 10

32. In the last three years, how many persons have you personally won to Christ (excluding your own children) who now attend this church at least once a month? _____
33. How long ago did you finalize your decision to trust Christ as Savior? _____ years

34. Three years ago, the phase of spiritual life I was in was best characterized by the statements in
    a. questions 1–10 (or I was not a Christian three years ago)
    b. questions 11–17
    c. questions 18–24
    d. questions 25–26

35. During the last six months, I feel my spiritual life and commitment to Christ, as evidenced by my changed behavior, has been
    a. quickly sliding backward
    b. slowly sliding backward
    c. staying about the same
    d. growing slowly
    e. growing quickly

36. My present feeling about my spiritual life is:
    a. I'm dissatisfied with my growth but am not committed enough to do anything about it.
    b. I'm dissatisfied with my spiritual growth and truly want to grow more.
    c. I'm satisfied with my present spiritual growth rate.
    d. I'm growing too fast and need a slower pace.

Table 8 continued

155

What Impact Looks Like
Overall Progress
Chicago T-NET Final Results from 21 Churches

Church Name_____ City_____ Pastor's Name_____ Today's Date_____

Please quickly read each statement below. After each statement, indicate in the first column the percent of that activity your church had completed before it entered T-NET. In column two, please indicate the percent of that activity which your church has completed at this time. In Questions 22–28 use numbers of persons rather than percentages.

Activity	% Complete		
	Before T-NET	Now	Change
1. Developed a clear, measurable definition of the disciple you are trying to make	14	85	+74
2. Developed a good understanding of the philosophy and purpose of a disciple-making church	16	78	+62
3. Made a commitment as a small core group of leaders to disciple making as the primary purpose of your church	23	86	+63
4. Voted as a congregation to adopt a specific disciple-making philosophy of ministry	9	93	+84
5. Voted as a congregation to adopt this philosophy of ministry	2	75	+73
6. Started at least one "model basic accountability group"	22	91	+69
7. Finished this model basic accountability group and deployed graduates as group leaders	17	77	+60
8. Started a leadership community of "some kind"	8	74	+66
9. Started a leadership community that meets at least twice a month and includes only "Be with Me" disciples in agreement with your philosophy of ministry	5	55	+50
10. Started more than one "level" of small groups with qualified leaders	14	61	+47
11. Started at least one proactive open group either an ABF or small group	39	84	+45
12. Started several truly open groups that are growing numerically	33	60	+27
13. Launched a disciple-making children's ministry project as taught in T-NET	8	49	+41
14. Included ABF leaders or other subgroups in your leadership community	6	32	+26
15. Implemented spontaneous evangelism approaches that won adults to Christ and your church	16	42	+26
16. Implemented strategic evangelism approaches that won adults to Christ and your church	30	45	+15
17. Developed effective assimilation strategies	20	47	+27
18. Began to develop standardized apprentice training curriculum	2	38	+36
19. Made structural changes or discontinued programs that hindered disciple making	12	49	+37
20. Caused a few people to get angry and leave	19	24	+42
21. Caused quite a few people to get excited and involved in disciple making	13	55	+42

	# Persons		
	Before T-NET	Now	Change
22. Number of adults won to Christ and your church in the two-year period preceding T-NET compared to number won in two years of T-NET attendance	3	6	170%
23. Number of persons in your church in the "Come and See" stage	78	86	156%
24. Number of persons in the "Follow Me" stage (at least in BAG)	32	51	562%
25. Number of persons in the "Be with Me" stage (finished BAG and involved in ministry)	19	26	285%
26. Number of persons in the "Remain in Me" stage (reproducing disciple makers)	7	11	232%
27. Your average worship attendance (inc. children) over the last three months preceding T-NET compared to your average worship attendance in the last three months now	349	406	18%
28. Est # of persons practicing and growing in disciple-making behavior in your church before T-NET compared to now	19	48	510%

29. Was T-NET worth the time and money you invested?
a. Definitely Not 0%   b. No 0%   c. Unsure 0%   d. Yes 57%   e. Definitely Yes 43%

Table 9

Though a noble intent may start the program, it becomes ineffective when church leaders are faced with the reality of their congregation. Randomly developing a program without information about your church is very much like sending your child to a school without any sequence. Start your daughter in the seventh grade, then take her to second grade, then jump to the twelfth grade. No parent would put up with such nonsense, so why does the church? Understand your church before you try to fix it!

Stepping-Stone 5: Apply Principles of Change

Without training, most leaders try to change people and organizations according to their own personality type. While I have been tempered by time, the Holy Spirit, and experience, I remain controlling, impatient, opinionated, and confident. My method for leading a church through change was to present the change from the pulpit, convince the board

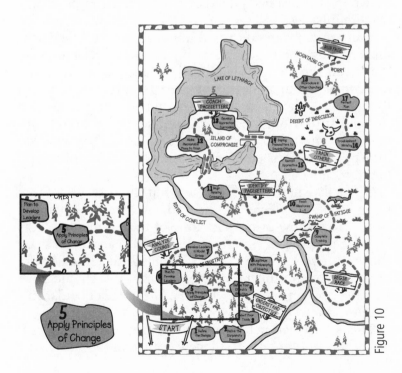

Figure 10

Four things can be changed in the church environment: behavior, structures, technology, and values.

to move ahead, then do it. This created conflict that I would proceed to knock down by strength of personality and just being tougher than my opponents.

This is called the "scorched earth" school of change. It isn't taught in any school and it doesn't need to be; it's as natural as wanting to rule the world. If I knew then what I now understand, I could have saved myself and others a lot of unnecessary pain. You will note I said "unnecessary pain," I didn't say *all* pain, because change always leads to some corporate pain.

I had a better idea for our church and my time than for me to teach the Wednesday evening prayer service. We started with fifty people in attendance at our prayer service, out of a church of six hundred. After a year I had it down to twenty; the rest had joined our new small groups or outreach ministries.

I very much wanted to start a home group for new people. I proposed to the executive board that the deacons take the prayer service. This would allow Jane and me to host a newcomers group in our home once a week. It passed with flying colors; the entire thirty-person board considered it a brilliant stroke. But the next day phones began to ring, not my office phone but those of longtime power brokers who didn't like the decisions. This included the wives of several board members.

Officially I never heard a word, but the first week I was not present, the chapel was packed with nearly sixty upset people in a show of power. None of these unhappy folks had attended the service in the time I had been pastor. Then they sent two envoys who had attended the church for at least a decade to our newcomers group. You should have seen the newcomers' faces when the fifteen-year board member introduced himself.

This all seemed petty and strange behavior, things real Christians wouldn't do. (I still believe that for the most part.)

I realized sometime later that my idea was good and right, but my method had been wrong. I learned that before a church can change methods or programs, it must change values. The executive board understood the value behind my decision; the other group did not, because they were not included in the change process.

Understanding a few facts about change can help us be leaders instead of martyrs.

Know What You Can Change

Four things can be changed in the church environment: behavior, structures, technology, and values. But please don't try to change the first three without addressing values first. Many strong leaders have changed behaviors, structures, and technology only to have it all snap back to its previous arrangements because they didn't reaffirm or change the congregational values. Able leaders can hold a door open and let change in, but unless they address values as soon as they let go of the door, the hydraulic hinge promptly closes it. Church values begin with doctrinal beliefs, then roles of the staff and its members, and the interface between congregation and culture are next. Often the challenge is not to change values but to remind everyone of the good ones they have already agreed on. Then a leader can develop people's understanding of better ways to realize the fulfillment of those values.

Know Your Church's Structural Age

The calendar doesn't always give you an accurate measure of a church's age. I served in a fifteen-year-old congregation that was structurally one hundred years old. It had been cloned from a church that was eighty-five years old. Its customs and reasons were rooted in the founding members and their memories of the mother church. Younger and newer members, who had no such memory, found themselves in a difficult situation.

159

We use the chart Five Stages in the Life Cycle of Churches in our training because it reveals where your congregation is in its life cycle. Once leaders have identified the stage their church is in, they can determine how to approach change in the best way and avoid unnecessary conflict.

Another helpful tool is Adizes' *Corporate Life Cycle*. It points out the best time for renewal and also when it is too late. As you can tell from figure 11, from Adolescence to Early Bureaucracy are the best chances for renewal. The optimum time however is a just after the organization has reached maturity. At these times a church is stable enough to handle change with minimum conflict.

Be Proactive

Because all organizations expand and take on "water," they need constant attention. The wise approach is to annually evaluate all methods and programs. Be ruthless, take no prisoners, and be willing to change with the goal of living out and affirming your values. In any organization I have led, there is annual evaluation and change. Our church elders would go on retreat twice a year to do such work. Annually we would write out every function required to live out

Adizes' Corporate Life Cycle

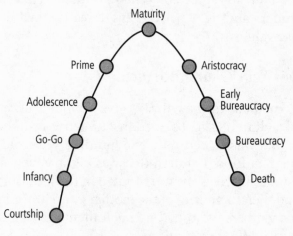

From Adizes', *Corporate Life Cycles* (Englewood Cliffs, N.J.: Prentice Hall, 1988).

Figure 11

Five Stages in the Life Cycle of Churches

	1 Initial Structuring Stage	2 Formal Organization Stage	3 Maximum Efficiency Stage	4 Institutionalization Stage	5 Disintegration Stage
Understanding of Purpose	Everyone understands clearly	Everyone understands clearly	Large majority understand clearly	Purpose is outlived or forgotten	Purpose is survival
Goals and Programs	Not yet developed	Developed and carried out	Clearly seen and carried out	Major focus of church	Irrelevant to meeting needs
Communication and Organizational Structures	Not yet developed	Mostly loose-cannon style below the board level	Developed and coordinated	Well established and coordinated	A church tradition
Attitude toward Change	Members receptive Change is instant Initiated at all levels Very little opposition	Members receptive Change is quick Initiated at all levels Very little opposition	Members mostly receptive Beneficial proposals always considered People follow leaders	Members not receptive Few changes proposed No major changes pass without bloodshed	Can't be done Change is a threat to existence We've never done it that way before
Membership Involvement	Everyone involved All willing to work	High percentage involved Volunteers easily found	Over 60% involved Enthusiasm high for participation	40% do 90% of the work; original members "retire"; volunteers serve by guilt	10% do 90% of the work; people volunteer only to survive
Morale	Morale is high Faith is high	Morale is higher Hope is high	Morale is highest Confidence is high	Morale polarizes into high and low Tradition is high	10% are determined, 90% despair Frustration high

Table 10

our mission. Then we would closely evaluate the effectiveness of each method or form we used. We would assign different elders different tasks each year, based on their skills and how God was leading them.

If you make change a normal part of your organizational culture, you will be able to keep the organization in the maturity region, according to Adizes' Life Cycle.

Five Steps to Change

I am indebted to my colleague Bob Gilliam for developing the five steps to change. While I have adapted them, the seeds were sown by Bob. Our Training Network 1,000-day reformation journey teaches this in great detail. There is no substitute for the opportunity to be coached through this process.

Step one: Create discontent. Creating discontent is not the same as creating trouble. Creating discontent is introducing the problem: "Ladies and gentlemen, we have a three hundred thousand–dollar budget, three pastors, and 275 regular attendees, and last year we recorded one adult conversion." Now that's a problem! This begins a discussion from the pulpit as to the strength or anemia of the church. You as leader frame the issue and support it with Scripture. Do *not* blame the congregation, because this is usually a leadership issue and a structural problem. The most crucial act is for the leader to affirm the good value of reaching people and demonstrate the discontent that everyone feels as a result. Then the congregation will begin asking, "What do we change?"

Step two: Gather some advocates. It is so sad to see leaders who stick their necks out with a sermon or take a prophetic stance only to learn no one is following. Gathering "true believers" is crucial to success in any effort to transform. Finding the highly passionate follower is a frustrating and empty enterprise. You don't *find* advocates, you *develop* them.

In my ministry, whenever I have determined that change was needed I first considered the price tag. At any given time many things need fixing and they must be prioritized by both importance and cost. Number one on many pastors' "wish list" is ridding themselves of the Sunday evening service. Another wish may be to transform adult Sunday school classes from being cognitively driven to relational communities with a teaching element. Both are important, but the pastor discerns that discontinuing the Sunday evening service could require the ultimate sacrifice, his job. The wise choice then is the adult Sunday school. The reaction to this change may be more positive, because it does not require ending something, but improving it. Even at that, this task will require great skill and perseverance, and the pastor will need help.

You don't find advocates, you develop them.

The best way to gather advocates is to identify kindred spirits in the natural flow of ministry. I trained future leaders to think by teaching them in the crucible of church life. I would point out a real situation and then teach them to ask common-sense questions. It was always a joy to see leaders that I had trained asking the tough questions, taking on the difficult situations, and succeeding.

"Where do you think George got that opinion about evangelism?" I would ask. We would talk about the genesis of strange antiscriptural attitudes among long-standing church leaders. We marveled at how well meaning many were, and how wrong they were. We set out to change their minds and to transform the church.

The first meeting I had with a group of five young men on the first day of my first pastorate is instructive. I began by telling them that I was not sure how things would work out, but if we trusted God and stuck together, we would succeed. We considered ourselves the "young lions" with a mission. It was life's most important mission, leading others to a deeper relationship with God and then leading many to know God.

I've never seen businessmen work so hard in their free time. They considered it an honor just to get to do all this neat stuff. They were willing to take on the tough assignments. They liked it when they could handle the opposition and protect me. A pastor can have advisors—or he can train advocates.

163

Step three: Prepare for conflict. By creating discontent and gathering advocates, you have made the situation liquid. It is unfrozen. Now change is possible. You prepare the troops by telling them that some conflict is normal. There will always be late adapters, along with some that never adjust to change. The reason is simple: some people don't want to lose familiarity and power.

I had labored as pastor in a troubled congregation for three and a half years. By then I had found favor with most of the membership. In fact I could get 90 percent of the vote on any subject. But I felt that the 10 percent who started the church deserved the right to be heard. I recommended a solutions committee be formed, three members to represent the 90 percent and three for the 10 percent. That is fair; it is also stupid. They were to discuss the new philosophical architecture that I had developed. The committee met several times, and each meeting stretched past midnight. After several meetings the committee submitted their report with eleven recommendations. They were so appallingly superficial I could hardly believe my eyes.

The best policy is to have nothing to hide; there are no secrets with respect to policy, procedures, programs, and proposals.

Here are a few for your reading pleasure:

1. Mention people by name in your pastoral prayer.
2. Return to the Wednesday evening prayer service.
3. Be more supportive of denominational programs.
4. Spend equal time with people; don't focus so much on leaders.

The enemy's strategy was to throw in the way of my ministry traditional expectational roadblocks. Oh yes, one of the eleven recommendations was "Stop talking about making disciples so much." It's interesting how any act can be misconstrued. A pastor may require leaders to be trained, and it is labeled "picking only your favorites." A pastor may focus on outreach and be accused of "neglecting the saints." Questioning the purpose and productivity of long-standing programs is "lacking respect for the past."

Many times people cease to be rational; they simply assign blame and then choose up sides. I have been accused of dismissing the need to visit a little girl struck by a car and of not caring about people because I didn't leave my office door open. I was seen dancing and drinking at the local country club. With what they paid me, how could I get into a country club?

Okay, I did lock my office door. Guilty as charged.

Enough of my problems! The question is how do you avoid conflict? You can't! But you can reduce its negative impact. Communicate openly with those who resist change. Don't present information to them as done deals; present it as discussion points, things to think about or even to pray about. Don't surprise them, treat them fairly and kindly, and more than anything, love them. Allow them to discuss issues in informal settings. Create discussion groups and forums. The mistake churches make is developing great ideas and programs behind closed doors. Then they announce an official meeting, drop the bomb, and take a vote. In this scenario the people will not act rationally; they will react emotionally. The general rule should be that by the time the vote is taken, everybody is talked out and everyone knows how it will turn out.

The best policy is to have nothing to hide; there are no secrets with respect to policy, procedures, programs, and proposals. There will still be disagreements, but no one will be taken by surprise. It will be a respectful environment, and the leaders will be considered teachable and open. It has never failed that such discussion has created a better decision. As Peter Drucker says, "All good decisions include disagreement."

Step four: Make the change. You have unfrozen the situation and prepared for conflict; now you can make the change. This simply means you implement the plan. You will need to establish procedures and provide personnel and funding.

On one occasion, after a good deal of conflict, I was able to implement an outreach program along with the funds to make it work. The key to all this was that I had clearly communicated the plan to church authorities and had it included in the budget. When the steps are taken in order, changes can be made.

Step five: Make it official. This could be called the refreeze stage. For anything to last at least ten years, you must provide structure. Sometimes that structure is a dedicated space; it could be new staff or an innovative task force that gets plenty of press in the church newsletter. At times it may require a bylaws change.

I wanted the church bylaws to state that no one who had not completed our training program could be considered for eldership. That would make it official, part of the corporate culture. It could be included in the long-range planning or be included in any new church literature. The point is to make the change on the marquee. It is now part of us.

Stepping-Stone 6: Plan to Develop Leaders

It is commonly held in the National Football League that former San Francisco Forty-Niner coach Bill Walsh is an offensive genius. He led his team to four world championships during the eighties. One of Walsh's methods that has been widely adopted is scripting the first twenty-five offensive plays of a game. This fixes a strategy in the minds of the players and gives the quarterback a studied confidence during the first quarter. Yes, there are games in which the plan has to be changed quickly because of a fumble and interception, but generally the plan is followed successfully.

All good coaches have a very well-prepared game plan, but the best coaches have the ability to make adjustments, especially at halftime. Electronics have made it possible for coaching staffs to make immediate adjustments play by play. Several coaches on the sidelines wear earphones so they can communicate with their staff in booths high above the playing field. Constant recommendations and evaluations are made concerning the next offensive play or defensive alignment.

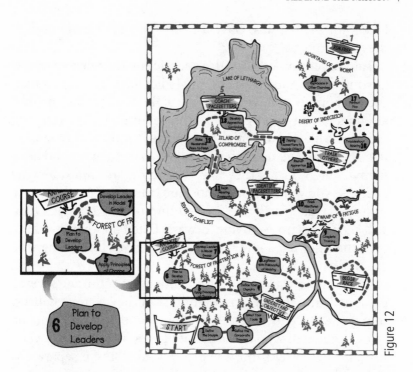

Figure 12

Leadership requires a simple plan along with a willingness to make adjustments as you go, based on game conditions.

This is why I am not a fan of long-range strategic planning. Such plans rarely get used, and they become out of date when your key leader is injured, or the deacons turn the ball over for the third time in the month. Use pencil to write your plans. The best leaders are always prepared and operate on principles rather than on fixed plans. A plan gives you only a template on which to think and make adjustments. Forming a plan for developing leaders should be principle based, flexible, and friendly to adaptation.

Know the Assignment

I have spent much of my life seeking leaders. What I don't do, however, is look for the finished product. I look for eagerness, for that light in the eyes when the challenge of ministry is discussed. I am drawn to the person who has the aptitude for discussing issues, who asks the right questions.

167

I look for people who have a heart for what we are doing; they are hungry.

I almost always begin with a generic small group and invite anyone who wants to attend. My belief has always been that the ones motivated will come. Usually two kinds of people attend such an open group in the beginning of a ministry: those who like power and those who like ministry. People who talk about how many conferences they have attended and how many church boards they have served on are almost always *not* those you want. Their agendas are laden with much church baggage. They usually are locked into older paradigms that will keep them from moving forward. Often they have the attitude that they are doing you and God a favor by helping you out in their spare time.

I remember a group I started with a new church. Several seasoned church veterans attended but they weren't willing to pay the price to start and lead new groups. I took note of two young men who demonstrated humility and were very hungry. Two weeks into the group I asked them separately to have lunch with me. That began their training and preparation for the future. They were both businessmen at the time. One is now a missionary, the other a lay preacher and very effective leader. I knew the assignment was to start new groups and attract people. I knew leaders need to be hungry and eager to learn, and these two were. I scripted my first plays and then adjusted as the group continued.

Provide Vehicles for Training

The vehicle that can train leaders must simultaneously multiply leaders and meet the needs of ordinary believers. This vehicle is normally a group of some size involved in the flow of congregational life. By virtue of the group's nature it should train the leader to lead. Normally you start would-be leaders with an easy assignment like a six-week group that will study how to be a better parent. There's nothing easy about being a parent, but the group is not complicated. People come when they can; they do homework if they want; it lasts six weeks.

The new leaders don't have to provide discipline or build community in the short-term group.

The group should multiply leaders as the leader picks another person in the group to eventually replace himself. He talks with the person and does the same thing in training with that individual that I did with him.

Finally, the group should help the members who attend, in this case helping them become better parents. It should give them a place to pour out their hearts, get support, and learn some helpful principles.

> The best way to keep vision alive is to keep it simple and make it clear.

Communicate the Long-Range Plan

The best way to keep vision alive is to keep it simple and make it clear. I normally would tell the entire congregation about our plan. "Ladies and gentlemen, we have a plan for taking you on the journey to spiritual maturity and fruitfulness. You can start in short-term, open groups that are targeted to your most pressing needs and interests. As you progress, we have groups that are designed to develop the common characteristics that lead to important spiritual habits and ministry skills. These groups will be longer in time and require more of the members, because the payoff is bigger, but so is the investment. Then we have a series of groups that focus on outreach and using your God-given gifts to their maximum. This entire process will take a few years, but as in any school or experience, you will bear much fruit and enjoy the journey."

The leaders need to think through the reasons for every group and understand how they, as leaders, can work their way through the process. A church member works through the system as a member; the new leader's training is working through the process as a leader. This process of developing a top-notch leader takes around five years.

Again, when you know what you are trying to accomplish, then you can build a very effective leadership procedure on broad principles.[4]

169

Major Barrier: The Forest of Frustration

Today I am in the forest of frustration. I write at an L-shaped desk, covered from end to end with the five major projects in which I am engrossed. The disarray on my desk is a metaphor for the clutter in my mind as I try to keep it all straight. Some days my mind races from one project to another, and I debate within myself as to where to pour my energy. Sometimes I want to jump to my feet and scream but then I go play golf instead. There is something about chasing a little white ball and hitting it hundreds of times (many of which I count) that clears the head and rids me of frustration.

But for readers who aren't into such self-flagellation, here is another solution. When I get frustrated with the many projects, I think of the axiom that you chop down a forest one tree at a time. Sometimes you can't see the trees for the forest. First, I prioritize the projects, then I assign each one its proper place in my schedule (daily) and the calendar (monthly). Then for the hard part: I stick to it. Writing this book took several months of hard and frustrating work. I simply set daily, weekly, and monthly goals. I disciplined myself to finish certain sections by certain times; then they found their way into my daily agenda.

A pastor looks at the first two milestones and says, "This is a lot of work!" The frustration comes when the scripted game plan is interrupted by a few "turnovers." People don't do what they said they would. Opposition is created by the left out or the uninformed. The frustration is best challenged first by prayer, then by a simple plan that organizes the project. There need to be clear deadlines, assignments, and accountability. This is all driven by the vision of the finished product and how it will take the church forward.

When you are able to handle your frustration, you can move ahead with perseverance.

Redesign
Your Infrastructure 8

Milestone 3: Begin the Race

The preparation is complete, and the race begins. Now you draw attention to yourself. You go public. I have vivid memories of this stage of renewal in one church I served. I had preached my theories and ideas for nearly a year and had quietly laid the groundwork for renewal. People patted me on the back, shook my hand, and told me of their admiration for my challenging sermons. I have always found it such a mystery that a pastor can say the most radical things from the pulpit with scriptural backing, and people not only accept them but extol them. But when I proposed the same ideas in practice to the board of directors, they responded as though it was the first time they had ever heard them.

171

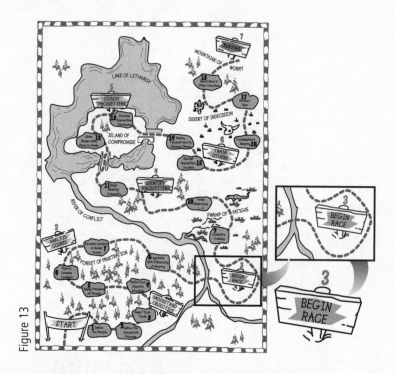

Figure 13

And it was! Yes, in that context and with the prospect that it would change their lives, they resisted. You can blow off a sermon with a smile and a handshake, but an executive decision that requires money, time, and support is very different. People love progress and hate change, but you must run the race. Now that you know the course and have your objective in sight, get going.

The Box

If your mission is sacred and it has been redefined as an all-out rescue of the world, then anything standing in the way must be removed. There seems to be an intentional arrogance in the established church that says, "If God wins the world, he will run the mission through us."

I would retort, "That depends on us." If by *us* we mean organized churches only, then we have the same problem as first century Judaism, which held the same opinion. So when Jesus came, they refused to consider any authentic move of God outside their theological box. One of the most challenging issues in an effort to reform revived churches is getting them to think outside of the box.

If your mission is sacred and it has been redefined as an all-out rescue of the world, then anything standing in the way must be removed.

I have found no definition of the church I agree with more than Jim Petersen's in *Church without Walls:* "People who are indwelt by the Holy Spirit, who is transforming their character and giving them gifts they are to use for service. Every believer is to use whatever he or she has to serve one another—and his or her neighbors." Petersen goes on to present four factors that are necessary for the church to function:

1. Christ must be the head [authority].
2. The body must live in community [love].
3. There must be diversity of functions [growth and mobility].
4. All of this in the presence of the unbelieving world [outreach].[1]

A church does not need a lot of extras to be the "Real McCoy." What an intellectual feast the church would be if we were as creative as the Holy Spirit! What fertile soil for growing ideas and people! It would be so stimulating that it would attract people in touch with their culture, those who want to weave the gospel into the fabric of society.

The challenge for all reformers is that the box has become a bank vault, with the two-ton steel door, the combination, the timer, the alarm, and the difficult access. Every church's important papers and traditions can at first be kept in a large file folder, but then they must be moved to a filing cabinet, then to a small safe, and finally to a vault. The more precious

173

stuff a church takes on, the more sophisticated the alarm systems and the more difficult the access. Every time you try to get in, alarms go off, and a camera takes your picture.

The first step in breaking out of the box is to reduce what goes in it. If a leader can limit the necessities to the things that Petersen lists, then the box is open. But many churches have a closed system that only allows certain things in: only certain types of pastors, only certain kinds of music, and there are more taboos than initiatives. The breakout is changing mind-set concerning the roles of the pastor and of laity.

The Pastoral Role

I will not present or defend a particular pastoral role. I have done plenty of that in the *Disciple-Making Pastor* and in *Seven Steps to Transform Your Church*. The pathology of the institutional pastorate is the congregational mind-set that we pay him to be here for us. He is primarily then a chaplain, a counselor, a comfort to the ailing, a role model, a symbol of God during the key rituals at the entrance and exit of life. There is some truth in all that. Good pastors participate in all of the above. I believe, however, that all those roles are secondary to a much more preeminent role of preparing people to fulfill God's purpose in their life. He is to present the church with the creative tension between well-being and outreach. A good church always walks the tightrope, trying to keep a balance between self-interest and compassion for the world.

A reformed church needs a pastor who is willing to leave the closed system that insists on certain functions for self-authentication. For the clergy the hardest task is letting go of being needed, to no longer be the Bible answer man and guru of all wisdom. People go to the pastor for answers. He helps people with their immediate desires and needs, so he begins to think, *I minister and help, therefore, I am.* This is a very existential way for a pastor to live. He must step back from this kind of short-term validation and allow the larger role of educator to step forward.

Carl Jung describes the importance of such change:

> We seldom get rid of an evil merely by understanding its causes . . . and for all our insight, obstinate habits do not disappear until replaced by other habits. But habits are won only by exercise, and appropriate education is the sole means to this end. The patient must be drawn out of himself into other paths, which is the true meaning of "education," and this can be achieved only by an educative will . . . no amount of confession and no amount of explaining can make the crooked plant grow straight; it must be trained upon the trellis of the norm by the gardener's art.[2]

It amazes me that Carl Jung had a better grasp on biblical change than many Christian leaders. If revival and renewal come to the church, it will require change and that means structured and guided growth, bolstered by an educative will, shaped by the Holy Spirit. Getting out of the box means breaking down leadership to its principled non-negotiables and throwing away most of what we learned from church about what a pastor should be. Creativity can grow out of determined minds, temporarily stumped by the question, "What is a pastor or spiritual leader?" When people recognize that Scripture does not describe what we now call a professional pastor, it is the beginning of wisdom.

The Laity

"Ministry of the laity" is a cliché. Everybody knows about it, but almost no one knows what to do about it or how to make it work. It is somewhat surprising then how recent the emphasis actually is. In his research Loren Mead found no use of the phrase prior to the late 1930s. The first book on the subject in English was Hendrik Kraemer's *Theology of the Laity,* published in 1958. Mead makes the point that in the context of history, it is a brand-new idea. That is quite a gap—from the first-century Ephesian letter to Kraemer's work![3]

Training and releasing ministry to the laity is hard work. You have to pay attention to whether people are learning. The normal focus of ministry is for the clergy to work hard at doing duties well. If the pastor is doing well and preaching well, if the membership is up and finances are solid, then the church is doing fine. The laity take on a posture of political supporters who make their donations, serve on committees, and try to back up the pastor, to make him successful. So the credo of laity very often is, "When the pastor looks good, we look good." The laity can talk about their wonderful leader, their growing congregation, the stimulating sermons, the building program. They can be a part of something dynamic; it makes them feel as if they have done their part.

The clergy-focused paradigm must be turned on its head to become a laity-focused paradigm.

When the pastor moves to break the deal and change the paradigm, usually things fall apart. This is because roles begin to change. When the laity are confronted with being ordained ministers of the gospel, and the front door of the church is not just the way outside but the entrance to mission, change will be resisted, mostly from fear.

The clergy-focused paradigm must be turned on its head to become a laity-focused paradigm. Many well-meaning leaders would say that caring for the congregation is laity centered. That is true in the sense of pastoral care and relationships. But remember, unity is not built on relationships but rather on beliefs. Poor or damaged relationships can destroy unity but even good relationships cannot create the unity that brings about church growth. Its foundation is Christ and basic beliefs concerning his teachings. The church applies this by loving one another and loving others via outreach.

A laity-centered ministry pours all clerical energy into the laity's success and well-being. There is a symbiotic relationship between health and performance. The church needs both, but too often clergy forget the leadership factor when they measure how they are doing. How are the people doing? is the right question.

This change of focus calls for pastors to celebrate the ability of the congregation to live with integrity and to reach

seekers, even if their efforts do not translate into new attendees and make the church look better on Sunday. However,
the church does look better every other day of the week.

It takes a very courageous and emotionally secure leader
to let God and the congregation get the primary praise.

Stepping-Stones

There are two stepping-stones on the way to this milestone. They are: developing a small-group system and developing a philosophy of ministry.

Stepping-Stone 7: Develop Leaders in Model Group

By far the most flagrant mistake committed by churches
with regard to small groups is how they start them. In my

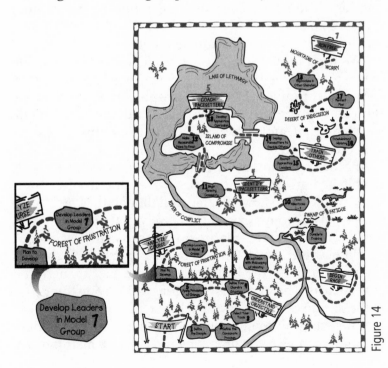

Figure 14

177

works *The Disciple-Making Pastor, The Disciple-Making Church,* and *Seven Steps to Transform Your Church,* I have outlined various ways to build a sequential and segmented small-group system. There are various kinds of small groups and almost endless materials that can be used in that context. The often forgotten or neglected aspect of small-group ministry is the principles around which it is built. Part six of *Seven Steps* in particular has helpful principles.

For now I want to focus on the challenges to reproducing small groups.

Common Mistakes Leaders Make

If you want to see long-standing multiplied renewal, the way you start is the most important factor. The most practiced mistake is to take a good small-group program idea with built-in materials and open it up to anyone interested. Sometimes this works for leadership training, but too often our methods of preparing group leaders give leadership training a bad name. The story I hear more than any other is one of good intentions, warm hearts, and great enthusiasm followed by great discouragement.

"We went to that seminar and came home 'fired up.' We issued a call to anyone wanting to lead a group to attend a Saturday training. Thirty-one people came out, and we started fifteen groups two weeks later. But the attrition rate was significant, and over the next twenty months the groups died out."

Another common story is an existing network of well-established groups that don't grow, reach out, or change. They are closed to newcomers, even though they pretend to be open. The groups exist for themselves, there is no intentional outreach, and there are no plans to start new groups or add new members. This of course is worse than the first example. At least the bad system in the first scenario no longer exists. That provides hope for starting something new. In the second case, you have a sick system that resists change.

When starting something new, asking yourself the right questions can save you problems and create something lasting. How often do I want to start over? What do I want to multiply? These questions address your objective and the intended product of your effort.

What kind of people are we trying to produce? By this point you have done all this work and it should not any longer be a mystery. How often do I want to start over? addresses the issue that unless you build well, you will need to start over again. Let me give you a formula for starting a solid, multiplying small-group system: Select your personnel; reproduce; have patience.

Select your personnel. I was new to the church and I knew there were three fronts on which I needed to work to renew the spiritual dynamic. First, I had to preach the values I held based on Scripture. Therefore, I started planting seeds that I hoped would grow into a great harvest. The second front was the church board. I asked permission to spend thirty minutes presenting my ideas and laying out my strategy to the recognized leaders. The third front, however, was to have the greatest impact, that was to start a small-group ministry. I knew that this could be added to the church structure without special meetings and votes, because people who would oppose such groups underestimate their power to transform lives. I knew the groups would create a positive revolution and by the time anyone thought to oppose them, it would be too late.

Yes, this was my profound strategy. I took three months to simply ask, "If you were going to start a small group, who would you choose to be your leader?" In a church of six hundred the same five names were mentioned multiple times.

The crucial element in this is to be patient and don't broadcast what you are thinking about. In the church I was in at that time, people would have been highly critical of selecting a special group of any kind without a three-hour business meeting with a lot of meaningless argument followed by a vote. Some traditions engage in adding to the sufferings of Christ through noble but misguided forms of self-flagellation—evangelicals just hold business meetings.

179

Reproduce. So I invited all five potential leaders and their spouses over for dinner. I told them only that I wanted to talk with them about a way to strengthen the church. After a very fine meal we gathered around the fireplace. I told them of my dream for the church and what we could accomplish in the community. I laid out my strategy of starting with a model group. I would do with them what I wanted them to do with others. We would meet once a week for six months and actually do the kind of group I wanted them to reproduce. I told them we would go one step at a time, that I would never ask them do anything I hadn't trained them to do. I gave them a week to pray. All five couples said yes, and we started two weeks later.

> *Model every kind of group you start.*

Six months later, all five couples had done well and were willing to start their own groups. We determined that we would start only three groups, and two couples would assist for a while. Each potential leader was given opportunity to learn how to lead the group, lead in outreach, and do all the activities necessary to success. The next fall we had three groups with fifteen members each, so forty-five people took part in small groups.

This is not good enough for many contemporary leaders, they want more, they want it fast, they want to microwave people.

Have patience. No leadership characteristic will help you more than patience. To be patient you must first get your ego into a harness. Impatience and impulsiveness destroy a lot of good works.

Answer the question, What do I want to have in five years? We generally overestimate the impact of one year and underestimate what can be accomplished in five. Six months after the start of three groups of forty-five, we started three more with apprentices out of the existing groups. Now we had six groups with more than ninety members. A year later the number was 150, and after five years over 500 adults had been through the groups. From that number we had trained fifty good leaders. Most of these leaders were now on church councils and leading ministries of various kinds. The entire dynamic and personality of the church had changed.

When you do it right, each generation of groups and leaders improves. This is because of various factors. But at its base, the model group done correctly will serve you well for many generations. Churches need various kinds of groups at different stages to target the multidimensional needs of the congregation. Each generation will improve as long as the basic principles are followed. Therefore, model every kind of group you start. This is the teacher's code. Every time you introduce a new kind of group or ministry, always have it modeled first. This will provide you with the base of operations for launching a multiplying ministry.

Stepping-Stone 8: Philosophy of Ministry

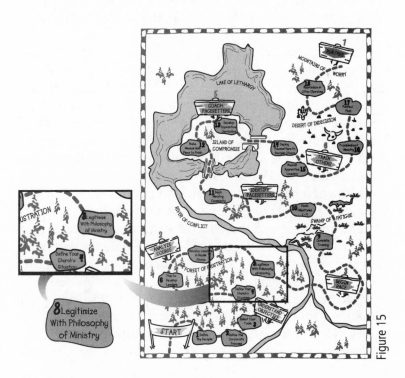

Figure 15

181

"Do two walk together unless they have agreed to do so?" (Amos 3:3).

You don't need a Ph.D. to have a philosophy. I used to think a philosophy of ministry was a very ennobling statement concerning my pastoral intentions. I later learned it is nothing more than a list of "the way we do things around here." Burger King has a philosophy. Everyone does. Some write it down—they are the ones who can articulate it.

Your philosophy is your methods and practices written out for the benefit of everyone, from visitors to board members.

Why Is Philosophy Important?

Church problems could be greatly reduced if churches would write out their philosophy of ministry. If I had understood this early in my pastoring, it would have saved me a lot of headaches. People spend a great deal of time debating trivial matters that are only issues because their methods and practices have not been written out and published churchwide.

I pastored three churches. In two I had a written philosophy of ministry. In those situations we didn't argue about the role of the pastor, the elders, why we had small groups, why we did evangelism off campus, or why we didn't have a Sunday evening service. When the pastor spent most of his time studying, writing, and working to develop leaders, people knew why. We understood that our church didn't exist to please everyone and it wasn't for everyone. It was not bad when people left our church or chose not to attend because they didn't like it. I encouraged people who wanted a Sunday evening service, choir, Awana, or whatever it happened to be to attend another church. If they wanted hymnals and so forth, many good churches in our community provide those services.

Some people think caring leadership is trying to provide something for everyone and compromising until everyone agrees. That is lousy leadership. You end up with a tepid congregation held hostage by the "sensitive" members. In fact those squeaky wheels are the worst kind of egomaniacs, who think other members should compromise their desires to meet their own needs.

Were we challenged? Oh yes! Many times newer attendees would take a run at us, especially those who were used to getting their way in previous situations. One of the better attacks was waged by a person who asked, "Is this church Bill Hull's serfdom?" He wanted to make me look like an autocrat because we had unity on what we did and why. He considered the church leaders yes-men because we agreed. He came from the "unless you fight a lot, you can't have a good church" mentality.

In fact our elders did have some heated disagreements, and I lost my share of arguments. But we always were one unit when we left the boardroom. We would not allow people to drive wedges between us. People who wanted to join our church or become leaders would be given our written philosophy of ministry. We didn't even pretend that we had a biblical justification for everything we did or for our method of doing it. We simply told them these were our methods of choice, and if they couldn't support and advocate them, they should not become members or leaders. Yes, this does hinder some growth, but numerical growth is not the highest value.

Reforming Your Philosophy of Ministry

By this point in the reformation journey you have clearly stated your purpose. You have defined your product. This forms the basis for your methods and practices. A philosophy of ministry is simply a list of ten to thirty statements of how you do things that is built on the foundation of your purpose and vision statements. The building blocks should be as follows:

1. State purpose.
2. Define product.
3. Define role of staff.
4. Define role of laity.

5. Define role of program structure.
6. List other helpful principles.

For more details on creating your purpose, philosophy, and principles, see Appendix B.

The role of your philosophy of ministry document in reformation is to give legitimacy to the changes you are making. Develop the document with church leaders in a workshop environment, then put it before the church board for approval and have it published for the education or approval of your congregation, depending on church size or polity. The educative role by far is most crucial in the long run.

This list of principles is a manifesto for revolution, a Magna Carta for leading the church into the future. It ends counterproductive arguments and starts productive ones. You stop debating the way the pastor is using his time or the style of worship and start debating the best ways to evangelize the community or how you will spend limited dollars in compassion ministry. Now *that's* worth debating.

Major Barrier: The River of Conflict

You may have seen the Robert Redford film, *A River Runs through It*. The film extols the virtues of a father having a common interest with his sons that holds them together as their life paths have separate directions. The river that runs through their land provides for the common love of fly-fishing.

The river that runs through a church during the process of change is the river of conflict. Conflict is a normal part of good decision making. What destroys communities of faith is not disagreement but anger, hostility, and a general lack of civility.

The greatest problem I had with conflict is I didn't like it. In fact I feared it because I feared the conclusions people would draw from it. I would think, *What did I do wrong?* Members of the church would automatically think of conflict as evil and that leadership were not doing their job.

Finally pastoral colleagues would speak of the conflict in hushed tones, "You know, Bill is having problems."

Now it seems all these responses were wrongheaded. Conflict can be a sign of health. It can be an indication that people are fully engaged and really care. The Doing-God's-Will-Is-Always-Peaceful school of thought obviously is not one that comes from the Bible. A much stronger argument can be made for conflict as normal than can be made for peace as normal. Unity does not require peace. Peace is something God promises the Christian as a matter of internal attitude. Peace between people depends on attitude and then the willingness to work out their differences. Thus you get unity.

Conflict is a normal part of good decision making.

I know a faithful leader will be opposed by the forces of darkness. He will be opposed by insecure and ignorant church members. The turf guarders and the carnal leaders all will come against any meaningful renewal. Anything that changes the power base will be fought. I now know that when conflict comes, it can be a sign of great leadership and God vigorously at work. I suggest we all get used to it if we want to be faithful and fruitful leaders. If we are filled with the Holy Spirit and help lead others through conflict to solution, we will be greatly used.

Milestone 4: Identify Pacesetters

Be careful, yes, be very careful! Many run but few should be chosen to set the pace for others. Pacesetters define normal, and their selection tells the church, "This is what we honor, like, esteem. It's our standard." A pacesetter has been proven faithful and is someone whom you would like to be a future leader. In the first test a pacesetter tries some limited leadership opportunity.

During my freshman year of high school I was required to take gym. The first day was a general evaluation of our

185

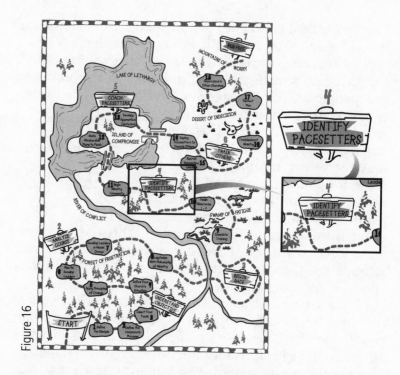

Figure 16

physical condition. I was among more than one hundred fourteen-year-old boys dressed in orange shirts and black shorts. We looked like a herd of candy corn. The mile run was the first assignment, and we all took off in an effort to impress one another that we could complete four laps around our quarter-mile cinder track. Some boys took off as fast as their young legs would carry them. It's impossible to evaluate one hundred boys dressed the same, bunched together on the track, during the first two hundred yards. By three hundred yards the imprudent fellows who had gone out in front were "gassed" and fell back into the pack. By the end of the first lap, the runners stretched out to fill half the loop. The coaches still had made no decisions. They only made humorous comments about those who started fast and were fading. In fact any serious coach was not yet serious at all. It was way too early to draw conclusions.

I find churches commonly choose as leaders "one-lap won-ders," who are out front after the first lap. Any track coach knows that the leader after the first lap is called a "rabbit." He sets the pace for only two laps, then drops out of the race.

New leadership selection frustrates many existing leaders because they made too many premature picks early in the race. Making choices early is attractive because it seems to remove the need for patience, thought, and the hard work of leadership development.

Runners bursting to the front in a long-distance race have already displayed poor judgment and a miscalculation of their ability. There are very few rules that I have adopted from my subjective experience, but one of them is as follows. *Persons who tell you after a first visit to your church that your message was the best they ever heard and that they have finally found their long-sought-after church home will never again be seen by you.* Yes, I know it is a very long rule, but it took me longer to accept. People who say such things are marginally unstable. Maybe one out of fifty follow through. Picking potential leaders too soon is just as unstable.

After two laps of the race the coaches begin to take notes. By now the runners are strung out around the entire oval and some of those early speed merchants are being lapped. Others are lying in the infield. The thoughtful and the strong are beginning to prevail. They have planned to pace themselves and save something for the finish. Now twenty-five boys are still running, and three are out front straining. As the final lap begins the prudent pick up the pace, and as they turn for home seventy-five also-rans in the infield cheer on their favorite.

When the race is over, God-given talent and strategy triumph. The race is over, and the coaches make their decisions. They group the runners according to ability, desire, and talents. The purpose will be to get the best they can from the one hundred boys. They will attempt to give them a physical education.

To identify ministry pacesetters, ask potential leaders to complete four assignments. Four assignments—four laps.

This may be simple tasks such as completing membership in a six-month group and becoming an apprentice in such a group for three more months. Add two short-term work projects like running the men's retreat or planning an outreach. The leader who completes this course could be considered a good candidate to have influence on others and to be a model.

Oh, by the way, I finished the race.

Stepping-Stones

The stepping-stones to this milestone include completing training and persevering through the four milestones.

Stepping-Stone 9: Complete Training

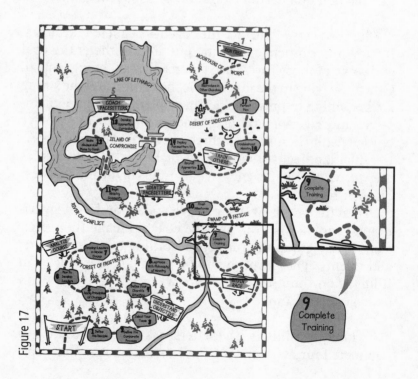

Figure 17

You make a pacesetter out of someone who has completed the training. This is simple and obvious, right? Then why is it so hard to stick to? Because tolerance is such a powerful force in our culture that it seems too rigid to create and enforce standards. This comes to the church in a slightly different package. A pastor hears phrases like, "We have to have compassion," "We are all sinners," "No one is perfect," and "We need to be patient."

I would not disagree with the above but I would remember that we are not told to be compassionate toward sloth or betrayal. We are actually told to "hold the line" on faithfulness to a task or quest (1 Cor. 4:2; 15:56; 2 Tim. 2:2). Whenever we break a scriptural principle we pay.

Lack of Commitment

"It ruins my whole day." These were the words of a very successful business leader in our congregation. I was hosting a 5:30 A.M. Bible study each Tuesday to start some potential pacesetters running laps. This man was a friend and highly respected among the members. He and his family had been very faithful to many of the church's ministries. But his faithfulness to church work had not developed real ministry skills. He did not practice spiritual disciplines, share his faith, or impact outsiders. My purpose in the early study was twofold: first, to introduce a new value system to the church; second, to "weed out" those whose motivation was simply to be in on things rather than the real issues of ministry.

This congenial friend came to me after four weeks (this is like one lap) and told me he didn't think he could continue unless we changed the meeting. He related to me how sleepy he got at work and how it destroyed his Tuesdays. I told him that every other person in attendance also hated getting up early and got sleepy too. But it was the only time when everyone could come and no one had an excuse.

I will never forget his honest words: "I guess the price is too high for me."

189

These are the moments when your flesh yearns to betray you. I wanted to make him feel good, to let him off the hook. I wanted him to stay with us. I was tempted to change the meeting time but I didn't. I let him walk away and return to the mediocrity of banal churchianity.

There are many, in fact most, who will walk when things get demanding. But please remember, if you don't let them walk early and you reduce demands just to keep them, they will later fold on you in crucial moments.

Willingness to Sacrifice

Same meeting, same day, same time—Tuesdays 5:30 A.M. The above potential pacesetter dropout left our meeting at 7:30 and drove three miles to work. Our second potential pacesetter left at 7:30 and drove sixty miles to Los Angeles. His words to me were, "You know, Bill, this meeting really makes my day!"

This man, whom we will call Carlos, had a heart on fire for God. To him, the meeting wasn't a sacrifice, it was a privilege. I have never met a layman who enjoyed ministry who wasn't overwhelmed with a sense of wonderment and privilege, "I get to do this stuff, to get in on what God is doing!"

Carlos became a small-group leader, then a leader of small-group leaders, and finally the most respected spiritual leader in the congregation. Now, more than twenty years later, he is still running the race, setting the pace for many younger runners. Carlos was willing to grow, had the humility to be trained, and the courage to try new and different things for God. I can't tell you how many times he stood with me in potentially dangerous times. He was someone I could count on to stand for truth.

I could count on him to oppose me if he thought I was wrong, and he did sometimes. When you train someone to stand for truth, you know the church is in good hands. You are sure that you are not surrounded by yes-men, but by courageous leaders of integrity who won't let even you, their mentor, lead them astray. I chose Carlos to be a pacesetter because he had successfully completed his training. He ran all the laps.

Stepping-Stone 10: Finish Milestones 1–4

The Wall

About this time in your reformation journey, you hit the infamous wall. The wall concept entered popular culture via distance running. Some say this wall appears at the thirteen-mile point; others think it comes sooner or later, but everyone believes in its existence. When you hit the wall, you feel like giving up, your mind plays tricks on you, and you can't focus on your original intent or goal.

In leading a church through the reformation journey, you hit the wall when you feel as if you are behind in accomplishing Milestones 1–4. Some people seem to understand the objective, but a number of important leaders have

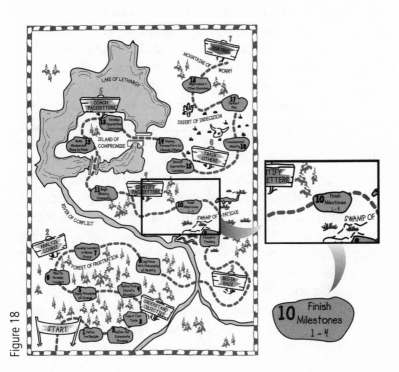

Figure 18

regressed to the previous paradigm. It was nice to be on the cutting edge, but now the great adventure is over. Back to reality. You understand the barriers and breakthroughs necessary, but there is just so much to do. You are attempting to develop the model group and refine your philosophy of ministry and you are exhausted.

When the Process Falls Apart

What makes your physical and mental exhaustion so difficult is the attacks that start unexpectedly from congregants who feel threatened. I just spoke with a pastor who has taken his church to the point of finishing Milestones 1–4. This is where you go back and make sure all systems are running well.

His first two years in the church had gone very well. Everyone appeared to be happy. One last thing needed to be done on Stepping-Stone 8, to legitimize the philosophy of ministry. His deacons and church staff had given their support. Then the document was mailed to the congregation. He spent four consecutive Sunday evenings explaining it but things were quickly falling apart. While opposition rose, Sunday evening attendance went down.

As you can tell, the opponents were not interested in understanding the document. They had made up their minds with the sharpness of those who take their stand on the King James Bible, forgetting that the Bible was not originally written in English. A good number of older members went on the attack (remember, most angry Christians don't play fair). Their attacks were on the leader's character, and they spiritualize their poison with phrases like, "He's been seduced by the spirit of the age." "He just wants big numbers." "He's taking our church away."

As a pastor, you are befuddled and ask, "What happened?" You sit at your desk, depressed and discouraged. You start thumbing thorough pastoral want ads. You call friends for "advice" but mostly for encouragement.

Facing the Challenge

You may remember the 1960s' television series *The Naked City*. Every program ended with the statement, "There are ten million stories in the Naked City, this has been one of them." The story I've just told is one of thousands of stories of the challenges to church renewal.

There are four routes to take in such a crisis. The first is to move ahead full speed; the second is to "back off" and pretend it didn't happen; the third is to quit. The first doesn't work because people just get madder. The second is a loser because the words have already been said, the accusations made, and people won't let you pretend. The third is wrong because it hurts everyone; no progress is made. A fourth approach often does work.

I suggested to my friend that he allow a short cooling-off period. This includes a conciliatory statement from the pastor, saying he and the leaders really believe this is the right course of action, but there is a lot of misunderstanding and they want to work things out. None of us really wants the enemy to win and to waste the next couple of years dealing with broken relationships and a lack of fruitfulness. So we are going to sit down and discuss the issues with anyone who is interested. If you are not interested enough to work this out, then you should have the personal integrity to disengage from the discussion and to not snipe from the stands.

Work it out in good faith, with the view that there is room for compromise and rewording of the document.

Oddly, the church my friend pastored was already practicing the philosophy of ministry, they just had not made it official. The natural question then is, Why make it public? Primarily leaders must understand that for the changes to stick through pastoral and leadership changes, the philosophy needs to be understood and endorsed by the congregation. Going public with the philosophy makes it harder for those charged with leading the church through change, but it pays big dividends later.

When you are headed to the promised land and are confronted by members who want you to back off from your

193

commitment to renewal, you may come on a major barrier to progress called the Swamp of Fatigue.

Major Barrier: The Swamp of Fatigue

The Swamp of Fatigue is when a leader experiences the cost of discipleship. The fatigue is battle fatigue due to opposition. It is emotional and physical as a result of work overload.

Stephen Covey in his book *First Things First* uses the image of a glass jar to make this point. He holds up a jar and puts as many large rocks in the jar as he can. Then he asks, "Is the jar full?" Some would say yes. Then he jams some sticks into the jar between the rocks. He keeps asking is the jar full. Then he proceeds to put in smaller rocks, then pebbles, then sand, and finally water.[4] This is what happens to leaders. They already have several major responsibilities, symbolized by the large rocks. As renewal becomes a priority, the sticks, smaller rocks, pebbles, sand, and water are added, which means more and more things to do. This is when a leader must stop and take stock of his life and priorities. It is difficult to do this until the leader is in the battle and the choices are real, not theoretical.

> *Making choices as to how you will spend your time and what activities will create the healthy, reproducing ministry are crucial decisions.*

Covey points out that the only way to reprioritize is to completely empty the jar and begin filling it again with large rocks. A very large rock will have to go in first. That's the only way it will fit. If you put all the same rocks back in, you have solved nothing. New priorities must be chosen if there is going to be real and lasting change.

This of course relates to the changes in leadership roles for the church. Making choices as to how you will spend your time and what activities will create the healthy, reproducing ministry are crucial decisions. It really isn't until this

194

point in the reformation journey that you must decide between wishes and desires. The priorities you choose at this point will shape your life for years to come. Have the courage of your convictions. Don't waste more time knocking yourself out for things you really don't believe in. Be honest with yourself and others.

Milestone 5: Coach the Pacesetters

A commitment to coaching selected pacesetters draws the line of demarcation from faithfulness to multiplication. This is the point in the reformation journey when most breakdowns occur. Most churches don't cross this line successfully. There are several reasons for this.

Administrative problems. The pastor has selected the pacesetters and has done basic training. But keeping track and up to date with what pacesetters are doing can prove too much

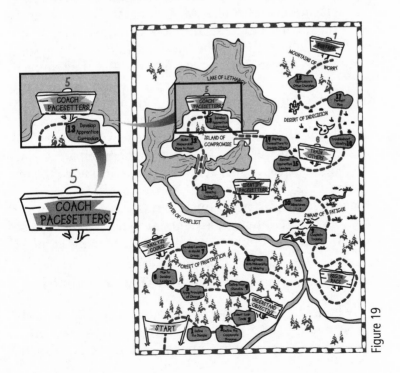

Figure 19

for a busy person's schedule—especially a schedule crammed with the traditional expectations and life's unexpected challenges. This takes us back to the importance of creating a working system that runs without a lot of maintenance.

Grooved in habits. One of the goals of every golfer is to possess a grooved swing plane that permits the maximum accurate force at impact. The good golfer does not overthink his swing. It is natural, and he just does it. Acting without overthinking has its advantages in golf, but when it comes to the use of a leader's time, some serious reflection is imperative. Church leaders become somewhat robotic in their use of time. This really traps the pastor who automatically starts meeting needs without asking, "Who else could meet this need?" "Who is best equipped to solve this problem?" It is tough for church leaders to turn over important stuff to others. But if pacesetters are going to consider themselves in other than a supporting role to clergy, they need to take responsibility in areas just as crucial as the clergy work.

Congregational resistance. Most congregations will resist becoming involved in doing the work of ministry. They don't mind so much being told they are ministers or taking some training in a targeted ministry skill area. But they do resist being on the same level as the clergy and most certainly don't want their pastor demoted by the promotion of everyone else. Coaching pacesetters means they will do premarital and marriage counseling, teach the new members class, baptize converts they lead to Christ, and participate in leadership of other sacrosanct activities once considered the private preserve of clergy.

Taking lay ministry seriously can be very turbulent and risky for church leaders. It is right, it is our calling, it pleases God, and it will be opposed. A solution is Stepping-Stone 11.

Stepping-Stone 11: Begin Ministry Community

My belief in a ministry community—a special time and environment that nurtures and trains leaders—grew out of observations I made during my pastoral years. The first ten

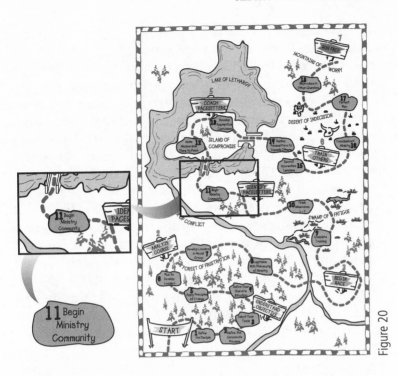

Figure 20

years I pastored I sat through a lot of inane meetings. The board chairman would call a meeting to order only to open a large black notebook passed on to him from the previous chairman. The only change anyone made was to buy bigger notebooks to hold the multiplying records. Yes, God was at work, people's lives were changed, progress was made, but it didn't need to be so banal. And there was no discernible link between the activities of the board and the church's fruitfulness. Such meetings were very much like punishment we all had to endure to do the work we loved. This made leadership trivial and boring, and the highly motivated avoided it like a tax audit. The real damage was that it placed well-meaning leaders into a trance, while church life remained in a state of suspended stupor.

During these years I had spent a lot of time developing highly motivated leaders who understood the church and had the skills to lead it. Having "cut their teeth" on leading

197

other seekers into a fruitful walk with Christ, they were passionate and willing to give a great deal of time and energy toward the ministry. This was so obvious to everyone that people began to nominate them for leadership positions, and they were elected to leadership. But within two years some of them were burned out. Because of the church environment they had lost much of their passion and were saying things like, "This is taking a lot out of me." They had never talked like this before.

It became quite apparent that most church systems only take from their leaders. They give very little, and the law of diminishing returns was the obvious result. One of the most dynamic and committed leaders told me after two years in leadership, "I can't believe how bad this has been. I won't ever get involved again. It has shaken my faith."

It's not always this bad, but experiences like this will get you thinking. I was committed to finding a way to build and nurture leaders. That is when we created the ministry community.

Paul's Example

The idea was really one part experience and one part Scripture. While teaching the Acts of the Apostles, I was impressed with the apostle Paul's leadership approach while in Ephesus. When he found the members of the synagogue unresponsive, even hostile, he took his faithful followers and went down the street to the lecture hall of Tyrannus. His motive was to spend his time in a more fruitful fashion, and one thing necessary to such activity is willing spirits. We are told he continued there for two years (Acts 19:8–10). There were several dimensions to Paul's ministry community. There was teaching. The community was fueled by passion and vision. They went out to minister and reproduce themselves.

Teaching. "He took the disciples with him and had discussions daily" (Acts 19:9). One gets the idea that under one roof they were having discussions concerning the truthfulness of the gospel and the ministry issues that confronted

them in reaching the region. This gave Paul's five basic followers—Luke, Aquila, Priscilla, Timothy, and Silas—the
opportunity to learn. Using the Socratic method of questioning, which required each person to defend a position,
Paul created an effective learning laboratory.

The most crucial thing about leaders is what they think,
so develop strong thinking in your leaders. Their convictions and understanding of
ministry and the church are far
more important than present
ministry skills. Ministry skills
can be developed in due course
by a well-grounded person.

Set the fire. The ministry
community is fueled by passion, vision, and a person with
the will to go forward. We met twice a month for two hours
each time. The first hour was always devoted to the spiritual development of the leaders. It was a shot of vision by
the leader.

> *The ministry community is fueled by passion, vision, and a person with the will to go forward.*

I often see senior pastors shy away from speaking at such
events twice a month. But this is as vital to success as the
Sunday sermon. The Sunday sermon is for the entire church,
but this other pulpit twice a month nourishes and challenges
leaders. There is no way to wire around the simple truth,
"As your leaders go, so goes your church." Pastors not seriously investing in leaders by both presence and preparation
will spend their ministry paying the price.

This was a time when I talked about both personal and
corporate leadership issues. We shared in communion and
prayer. We shared our needs and in solving our problems.
We didn't do that every week; we had to rotate the various
issues, but I always spoke to them for fifteen minutes from
my heart. This is how you keep your leaders nourished,
healthy, and motivated. If they are being helped, there is
added value to them in the relationships and the cause.

Application vehicles. If Paul's leaders had only talked and
debated, the results would have been very different. That
startling revelation is found in two easily missed words "so

199

that" (Acts 19:10). These words connect what they were doing to the evangelization of the entire province of Asia.

Never train anyone in a vacuum; it doesn't work. Clearly the team didn't spend all its time in the lecture hall. That would mean they were only half trained. It also means they would be much weaker leaders who probably would not discover their ministry strength.

Their evangelism reached its zenith in the starting of new churches and in a great impact in Ephesus (Acts 19:11, 18, 20; 20:20). They saw people healed. The thinking and practice of many people was purified. And six of the seven churches mentioned in Revelation 2–3 were started.

It is a crucial part of a ministry community to strategize together for outreach. Networks and church events are better crafted this way, and there is ownership on the part of the leadership. This also takes the pressure and expectation off the clergy to be the creator of all important ideas.

Provide an apprenticeship environment. During Paul's three years in Ephesus, twenty-seven people are named as having visited from other regions. The Bible names people and their hometowns. A scrupulous accounting reveals that at least one person from each region in which Paul preached and founded churches came to Ephesus for further training.

People who worked with Paul were expected to reproduce and multiply the gospel through others. This is easily documented in his pastoral letters (1 Tim. 3:1–5:17; 2 Tim. 2:2). Therefore, in the groups I've established, all members of the ministry community are required to reproduce by naming and training an apprentice annually.

How It Works

During the first hour of the community the entire group meets together. During the second hour, the community breaks down into huddles specific to their ministry assignment.[5] The more experienced leaders supervise various kinds of groups at different stages. This is the "nuts and bolts" of ministry and is just as crucial to the success of a future or existing leader as is the first hour. The apprentices are right in there with the other leaders, learning how to lead. At times for a few weeks they have special training in the ministry philosophy of the church. You can't expect them to advocate what they don't understand. It also serves them to own the vision and defend it in times of crisis.

The "sin" most often committed by those wanting to start the ministry community is to let the untested join. Before persons can join the community, they must really desire it and be qualified. We looked for the following:

1. They have desire (1 Tim. 3:1). If they don't really want it, don't waste your time.
2. They are passionate about the same things the leadership is. Do they identify with the mission and direction of the ministry?
3. They have gifts appropriate to the task—the aptitude and gifts to lead others.
4. They have been tested through some experience and have proven faithful to the membership of groups and to finish tasks previously assigned.
5. They are teachable. Do they really want to learn or do they have other motivation (they want to gain influence, don't want to be left out, or are just curious)?
6. They are emotionally stable. Have they demonstrated stability in human relationships?
7. They are needed. Don't flood the community with people you can't meaningfully train. If you don't have places to put them with respect to a ministry assignment, don't add them to the ministry community.

Some people will ask, "Can I just start coming and see if I like it?" If we are talking about anything but leadership, the answer to this question would be yes. One of my serious challenges as a pastor was being the doorkeeper to the ministry community. Many wanted to visit the meetings, and visiting was fine. We would let anyone come once to see what the ministry community was. But membership in it was not a look-and-join proposition.

I had two very strong personalities new to our church who learned that the real action was the ministry community. They asked to visit, and I told them that it was fine, but to join they would need to be an apprentice before they could be entrusted with any leadership role. They were aghast that men with their experience wouldn't be given honorary membership. They wanted to bypass the training and all the prerequisites required of all others. I told them we could not allow that for three reasons: First, it would be a breach of faith with those who had already earned their membership. Second, it would not be fair to them to thrust leadership on them before they were proven faithful and agreed with our philosophy of ministry. Third, their previous experience might be the wrong kind for our church culture, and time was needed for them to reveal the content of their hearts.

The basic rule of building a community is to pilot each kind of group, then manage those you have trained to lead others.

My parting word is don't get into a hurry to have a full-blown ministry community; that is, don't try to have many kinds of groups under various levels of leadership right away. Go slowly, stay faithful to your principles, and don't poison the pot by allowing the unqualified to become part of this special group. This should be separate from all official church boards, and the fact that someone is an elder or deacon is incidental. Elders or deacons are there because their ministry assignments are small- or middle-size groups or outreach task forces. The basic rule of building a community is to pilot each kind of group, then manage those you have trained to lead others. In the end you will have a system that ministers to the church populace, trains leaders, and allows leaders to expand their ministry base all in one place. It could start with one kind of group and five leaders. The five leaders of those groups would be a ministry community.

Then you have five leaders with apprentices, and in a few short years you will have many kinds of groups, and you will be in touch with them all through your leaders. That is leadership, discipleship, mentoring, and multiplication. It's a wonderful life when you do it God's way.

Stepping-Stone 12: Make Measurable Plans to Finish

Peter Drucker warns, "If you don't know precisely what results you are after, you're wasting your time."

I do not suggest becoming a slave to numbers, but there is a place for measurement. There is a time for us to give ourselves a reality check, to be honest with ourselves. I am not a big fan of strategic planning but I think annual goals of the right kind can be very helpful. A church is a process organization, and it takes so long to produce the product that you can get discouraged.

The first major mistake T-NET International made in working with churches was to have them write a plan at the begin-

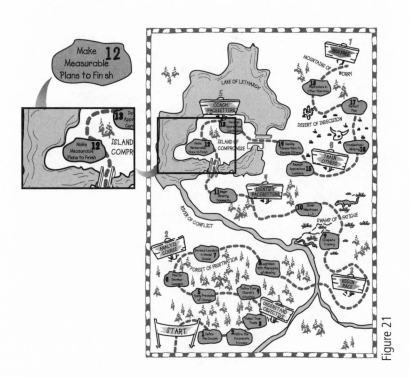

Figure 21

ning of the journey. But at that point they didn't have enough information. They didn't really know what they wanted. They had not established their core values. They were not unified philosophically. That is the reason we now wait until they have field-tested their ideas, and their convictions are "bone deep." Then they have what we call philosophical purity.

Goals are important because they provide a way for the team and the community to answer the question, "How are we doing?" To keep a positive attitude, it is crucial to keep records of short-term successes. This way you can build on successes and your passion will gradually increase. Without measurements that show progress, you open the door to discouragement and you don't have an answer for your critics.

What to Measure

Measure productivity rather than activity. Measure the things you truly value. I would reduce the importance of attendance as the zenith of all measurements. A church could be doing a very fine job of reaching and impacting people but not reflect this in new members. Attendance as the most important measurement is very cultural and very American.

I would measure such things as the number of new people entering the developmental system built to grow Christians, the number of new intentional groups, or the percentage of people moving into leadership. These are things you can actually control and can focus on for results. You can't really control attendance or finances.

I like what Christian Schwartz has done in his work *Natural Church Development*.

Schwartz advocates measuring activities that are within the reach of the membership to achieve. At the end of the year the entire congregation knows how they have done. The eight areas of leadership, ministry, spirituality, structures, worship service, small groups, evangelism, and relationships are the cardiovascular system of the church. Their well-being is a way to measure the health of the congregation.

There are many planning systems on the market. My only recommendation is find one that fits you and your church's temperament. Make a commitment to measure what you value and use a system that helps you know if you are getting the results you desire. Otherwise you are wasting your time. No one wants that.

Major Barrier: The Island of Compromise

Church culture does not accommodate this level of commitment to results on the part of church leadership. When a church becomes focused, especially before there is an abundance of results, people who don't like change will oppose the focus. Many feel more comfortable in leadership when there is no possible means of revealing failure. While success creates a need to innovate, failure can exist peacefully in a church for years. For up to twenty years a church can be sustained by donations of people who don't want serious challenges or changes to their way of life. They will pay for this with serious money. The pressure on leaders who advocate change is to back off or lose the financial base for their goals. The pressure is real, the money is real, but so are the goals and passions of the spiritual.

The course to take is what some have called the law of wing walking. That is, don't let go of what you have until you have a firm grip on something else. Change needs to be gradual, guarded, but moving steadily ahead. Even the threatened like positive results.

Reassign Personnel   9

It is time to give your congregation a new way of life, to deploy the trained and motivated into the harvest field. Now they know the door of the church is not just a way out; it is the door to the harvest field. The adventure of a lifetime, the challenge and fulfillment they are looking for are out there, not in here. People with a *redefined purpose* and a *redesigned church infrastructure* are now ready to be reassigned.

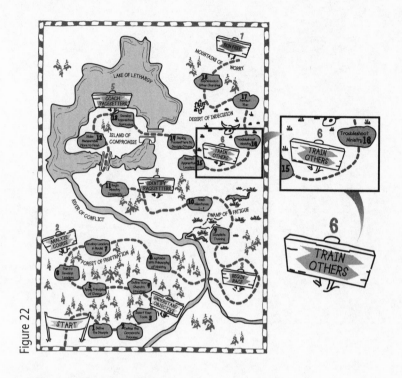

Figure 22

Milestone 6: Train Others

Training others to do the work of ministry *is* the work of ministry. The wonderful truth is that the person on the receiving end can't tell the difference. When I am in a store, sometimes I get waited on by a nervous young person with a smile frozen on her face. She is wearing a badge identifying her as a trainee. You know the service will be slow, but caring.

If Christians start going door to door with trainee badges, yes, the receiver will know, but this is not God's design. A small-group leader can be a trainee, but the group doesn't know, and the ministry is real, and God works. In fact all of us are training all our lives, and everyone in the community of faith is accountable to someone.

The energy of the community now turns to reproduction, working through others. The joy is that we have become a

208

community that impacts others to follow Christ, and the community members are impacted the most.

Compressed Stepping-Stones

Once you are down the renewal road this far, maintaining strict sequence of activity is impossible. Admittedly, much of Milestones 5–7 run together. It can be very much like spinning several plates. You have a sequence in starting them to spin but you must watch them carefully and go just at the right time to each plate and respin it at the proper time. Milestone 6 is training others; there are three stepping-stones that must be developed during this period. They are: develop apprentice curriculum, deploy pacesetters, and recruit apprentice leaders.

> *The door of the church is not just a way out; it is the door to the harvest field.*

Stepping-Stone 13: Develop Apprentice Curriculum

I am most often asked, "Do you have a curriculum for a ministry or leadership community?" My answer has always been, "None that you should use." Yes, every church should have a written set of materials for training apprentices in various areas. The best curriculum I know about anywhere is the one *you* write! It is based on principles that you hold dear and the philosophy of your church. Trying to take some other church's leadership curriculum and use it yourself is like trying to take another pastor's sermon notes and preach his sermon. It can be done, but not as well as doing your own. I would recommend reviewing every area of character and skill development and then building your curriculum as you go.

Anything written out of the soil of human experience in real time to that experience is always a superior document. This kind of document includes two ingredients not found

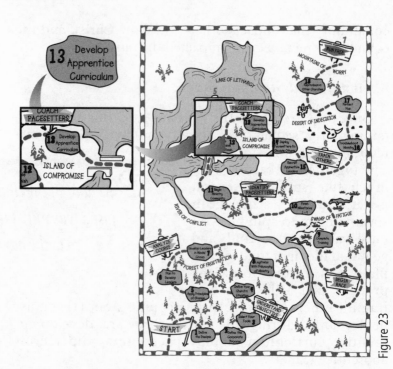

Figure 23

in books and other long pieces written in a short time: aggregate wisdom and field testing.

The two reasons to develop an apprentice curriculum are quality control and ease of multiplication. It takes a lot of duplication of effort to reissue a new set of instructions to every apprentice, especially since you are working through supervisors. As a pastor I was often introduced to new apprentices and had to trust that our supervisors were taking them through our agreed-on curriculum. You want both massive multiplication and confidence that your standards are holding strong to ensure the integrity of your work.

Stepping-Stone 14: Deploy Pacesetters to Disciple Others

This has already been done in a variety of ways, starting with the beginning of the model group. This simply means

210

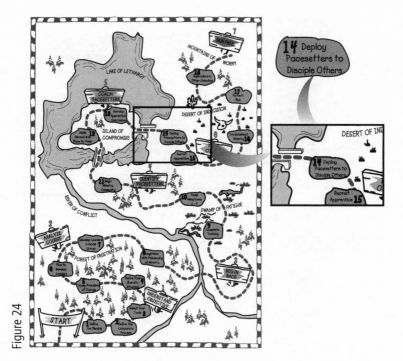

Figure 24

that now deployment is taking place on a churchwide basis, with various kinds and sizes of groups. It also means that there are always those whose creative juices precede your renewal sequence. I would recommend becoming their champion and turning them loose. This stepping-stone requires leaders to figure out basic deployment strategies with each group's or individual's ministry. This should take place naturally through your ministry community, and the supervisors should be doing it. The pastor would only read and comment on reports.

Stepping-Stone 15: Recruit Apprentice Leaders

This would already be the fourth generation of apprentice leaders. The first set of apprentices were the model group members. By the time you started ministry community, you had those original leaders plus their apprentices selected during the first months of their groups. Now you

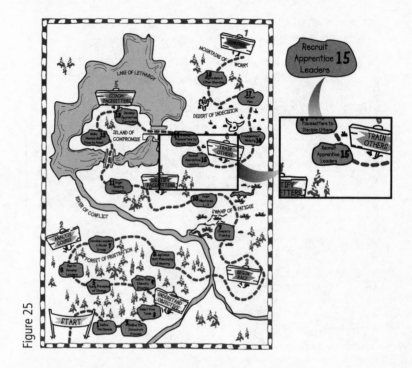

Figure 25

have the apprentices who were chosen by the model group members, who are leaders. The third generation of leaders now choose a fourth generation.

These three stepping-stones are really reruns of earlier ones, but now they involve more people and are more highly systematized. There is more training going on and it continues to multiply. Therefore, a well-organized system now will be necessary. Good systems will catapult you ahead for a multiplied harvest; bad ones will push you back into frustration. Without the proper organization, the weight of multiplication will cause your quality to collapse, and the end of fruitfulness will be near.

Major Barrier: Lake of Lethargy

Very often leaders just get overwhelmed and don't want to "grind" away at making this all work. Generally leaders find it difficult to sustain great organizational effort over several years.

The best cure for such normal propensities is to plan twice-a-year retreats for your community to recharge and build relationships. Bring in resource people who can add encouragement, not work. You can actually set yourself back by inviting an expert who is going to expose a weakness and "pile on" an already exhausted group. When you can have fun and play together, plus honestly address your challenges, it will do a great deal to bring the entire community out of its lethargy. Great accomplishment is usually the result of great effort made by ordinary people sticking to the plan that they really believe in.

Milestone 7: Run Free

According to Elton Trueblood, "Discipline is the price of freedom."

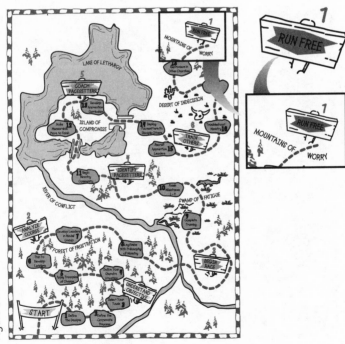

Figure 26

Freedom always has a price. For America it has been shedding the blood of our young through various wars. For those financially free, it was the disciplines of success and good planning. For the church, it is the discipline of creating a self-perpetuating system. In other words, the resources to keep the church growing and strong emerge as the product of the system itself. New leaders with new ideas replace the founders and subsequent generations: that is the picture of health. A church that is running free has worked hard with great discipline to give its members the structure to achieve their best.

Great accomplishment is usually the result of great effort made by ordinary people sticking to the plan that they really believe in.

Stepping-Stones 16 and 17: Troubleshoot Problems, Perfect Your Plan

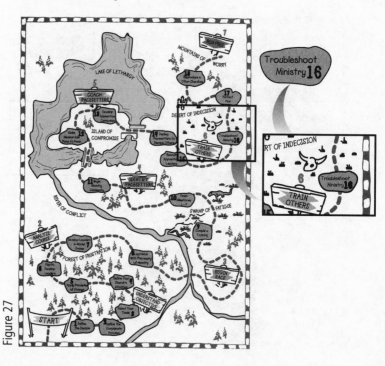

Figure 27

214

Just as important as building a system is maintenance of that system. Creative people are called to bring the vision to life and cut a new trail to both faithfulness and fruitfulness. Now enter the managers, the maximizers, the people who love to fix the broken. One problem that needs fixing at this stage is what to do with the variety of highly motivated people who are "inside workers" by gift and temperament. Did you know there are people who love to do the tedious jobs? They are the ones who like to help others work through problems.

You will look back at all the stepping-stones one at a time and notice breakdowns. The journey trail is clogged with dropouts and the struggling. This is when you **send in the counselors**, those who can provide what is needed by members to get moving again. One person (or a team would work as well) that is diagnostic in calling can do the job.

I recall a very heated board meeting when we were working each other over because of some unfinished and diffi-

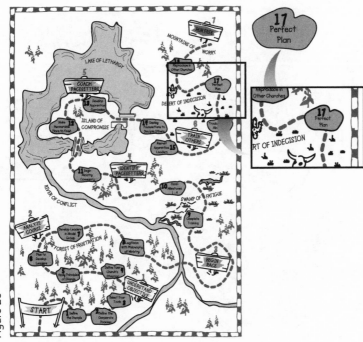

Figure 28

cult tasks. We were asking a couple of our members to take on tasks that would solve our problems. They resisted, and I was pressing them as to why.

Finally one man shouted, "Because that isn't me. I would rather have my arms chopped off than do that."

Given the example, we took him seriously and asked, "What would you like to do?"

To our surprise he wanted to do the difficult tasks, the dirty jobs that no one else liked. They just weren't the jobs we were asking him to do. What a glorious learning experience! We simply shifted to him some things that he wanted to do.

There are those gifted and called to inspect each stepping-stone on a quarterly basis and write thick reports. Then those gifted to fix the problems are discharged to do so. The community of Christ has all the people needed to both start and sustain the system.

Stepping-Stone 18: Reproduce in Other Churches

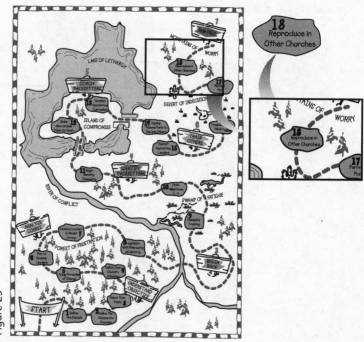

Figure 29

The best strategy for starting new, healthy congregations is to have them start from a healthy congregation. The most effective church planting strategy for a denomination is to restore repentant local congregations to health. When we started our transformational process six years ago most of the churches entering our training were not interested in starting a new church. It would be fair to say that most were convinced that they could not start one. They felt they didn't have enough people, enough money, or enough time. Nor did they have enough vision for reproducing themselves in the immediate community.

> *The best strategy for starting new, healthy congregations is to have them start from a healthy congregation.*

The wonderful news is that more than half of the churches that graduate from the 1,000-day journey leave with a vision and a plan for starting a new church. The change can be attributed to a reeducation of their responsibilities before God and their community.

It is too common for churches to be very inwardly focused and, let's admit it, selfish. I have often been bewildered by the congregation of two hundred located in a community of three hundred thousand resisting the planting of a church of their own denomination nearby. Every other denomination can come in, because there is nothing they can do to stop them. But if one of their own comes in, they protest, "This turf is mine." They don't even have the self-awareness to admit that they are reaching less than one-tenth of 1 percent of the population. Fishermen would never act that way. They go where the fish are. That is why you will see boats bunched together in a vast ocean. They are gathered where the fish are biting.

Restored churches desire to multiply themselves in the community to reach more and more seekers. They also want to pass on the benefits of their training by advocating that other churches join the transformational process. A church

217

runs free when its system is working, people are developing, leaders are produced, and some of those leaders go out and start outreach ministries. Much like the apostle Paul's strategy, they keep pushing out the edges of the places where the gospel is preached.

The two barriers that are potentially part of a leader's everyday life are the Desert of Indecision and the Mountains of Worry. The Desert of Indecision is symbolic of a lack of resources that you need to reach your goals. The Mountains of Worry represent the obstacles that arise between you and your dreams. As you run free in faith, you must be constantly reminded that God provides, like streams in the desert, the resources you need. He also moves mountains or will show you the way over them. Faith and courage are required to experience transformation.

Running Free Is the Starting Line

I want to leave you with five truths about your reformation journey.

1. *When you leave someone else's structure you must create your own.*
The journey map is only a guide to get started. You must create your own trail that is just for you.

2. *People will not internalize everything that is needed for spiritual health.*
Even the best-trained people fall at times along the way. Always provide lifelong accountability for everyone.

3. *The "flesh" does not improve.*
A truckload of knowledge and skill is no insurance against disaster. Chemistry among leaders is crucial, and please respect the power of the flesh even in the godly. We all are prone to go our own way. We need each other to help us keep our commitments to God.

4. *The bottom line is practice the spiritual disciplines.*

The more you can get people praying together, reading Scripture, living together in community, and interfacing with seekers, the more people will grow.

5. *You will be tempted to take an easier road.*
Don't.

The Church Needs Help and Health

My purpose in this book has been to call the church to a holistic view of spiritual awakening. For the church to be both faithful and fruitful, we will need a spiritual jump-start called revival and an ongoing process of change called reformation.

We may not know how or when God will send revival, but we do know that he calls us to be ready for him. Churches that make the Great Commandment and Great Commission their focus will be ready for the blessing, no matter what guise it comes in, whenever it does come.

The guidelines I have offered are only the starting line for the obedient church. Churches that are in position to obey God's commandments can experience a wonderful relationship with him that touches the entire community and society.

I pray that when he calls to you, you will hear his voice.

Appendix A

New Life Church
Philosophy of Ministry

Purpose: The purpose of New Life is to glorify God by making disciples who exalt God, edify other believers, evangelize starting in their own locale, and extend disciple making to all the world.

Philosophical Principles:

1. The purpose of every activity of our church is to produce and further develop disciples. We will evaluate every activity by its effectiveness in producing disciples, and will modify or discontinue activities that ineffectively do this.
2. We will, at all times, have an intentional strategy to accomplish each aspect of our purpose.
3. Evangelism (including pre-evangelism) is the starting point and indispensable catalyst to all disciple making.
4. We define a disciple as a believer who is becoming more like Christ by obediently growing in character, in ability to minister to others, and in helping to make more disciples.
5. We will primarily make disciples as a team, as a church, but not just as a collection of independent individuals.
6. The senior pastor's role and commitment is primarily to give direction, train leaders, teach the Word, and be a model disciple. He should seldom perform ministries lay leaders could do unless it is absolutely necessary.
7. The church member's role and commitment is to grow as a disciple, to be trained to use their gifts, and to be empowered by the Holy Spirit to directly minister to Christians and pre-Christians. The church will encourage and empower gifted individuals to be creative, proactive, need oriented, and decentralized in disciple making, and will grant permission and give resources whenever possible.
8. We will recognize servant gifts as being equally important as leadership gifts in building a healthy, disciple-making church.
9. All staff, policy makers, and group leaders must be growing disciples committed to the church's philosophy of ministry.
10. Leaders will be recognized by considering both character and giftedness.

11. We are committed to the principle of multiplication of ourselves by evangelizing, discipling, training, and delegating ministry to others who are faithful.
12. We will multiply ourselves and train others using the method of apprenticeship.
13. The primary method of making disciples is the decentralized small group. We see one-on-one approaches as valid, sometimes necessary, but only as a secondary method for most in our church.
14. Reasonable accountability is an indispensable method in making disciples.
15. We will offer nurturing/equipping ministries at multiple commitment levels to develop sequential growth for disciples.
16. Our evangelism will focus on multiple specific groups rather than using a generic approach.
17. Our organizational structure and leadership styles will flex and change as we move through our life cycle as a church.
18. We will promote the belief that the church's most important identity and ministry takes place while it is decentralized.

Area of Ministry	Examples of Qualitative Goals
Leadership	"By the end of the year, our pastor will be released from 20 percent of his regular responsibilities in order to dedicate this time to the training of lay workers"
Ministry	"At the end of nine months 80 percent of those attending worship services will have discovered their spiritual gifts and 50 percent will be active in a ministry corresponding to their gifts"
Spirituality	"By February 1 we will have decided which of the three lay workers under consideration will assume coordination of the prayer ministry"
Structures	"By the end of December this year, we will have determined a point person for each of the nine areas of ministry our church has established"
Worship Service	"From the beginning of next year, we will have a worship service each quarter that is specifically designed to reach non-Christians"
Small Groups	"Within the next six months, we will divide our home Bible study with the co-leader assuming the leadership of the new group."
Evangelism	"By the end of April the church leadership will have identified which 10 percent of the Christians God has blessed with the gift of evangelism and will have had a personal conversation with each one regarding this gift"
Relationships	"After having studied the 'Learning to Love Process' for three months, each home Bible study participant will agree with the statement: 'I am enjoying being a part of this fellowship more than in the past.'"

Appendix B

Purpose, Philosophy, and Principles

Bill Hull's White Paper

Purpose

To train leaders and transform churches to achieve their dream of significant spiritual impact, to transform the church worldwide, and to raise up a new generation of fruitful leaders.

Vision

Commitment to multiplying this passion for impact wherever God is at work, people are receptive, and technology permits.

General Description

Process

Parallel training is in process worldwide. Interest is generated by direct mail and personal invitation to a Leadership Briefing (breakfast or lunch meeting) and a One Day Warm-up (overview seminar).

The result is interdenominational participation with eight to thirty-five churches per site. Each church brings a team of people to be prepared to lead in "churchocentric" disciple making.

The focus is the 1,000-day Journey, with each team member focusing on one of three areas: leadership, education, or outreach.

Total investment in the process and supporting curricula during the last seven years exceeds three million dollars.

Impact

Seven hundred churches and six thousand leaders are now Running to Win, affecting more than one hundred thousand disciples.

Tangible progress will be made in key areas including sharpened church focus, numeric increase in small-group participation, decisions for Christ, and increased worship attendance.

Philosophy and Principles

Doctrinal Statement

We believe:

1. The Scriptures, both Old and New Testament, to be the inspired Word of God, without error in the original writings, the complete revelation of his will for the

salvation of men and women and the divine and final authority for Christian faith and life.

2. In one God, Creator of all things, infinitely perfect and externally existing in three persons: Father, Son, and Holy Spirit.

3. That Jesus Christ is true God and true man having been conceived of the Holy Spirit and born of the Virgin Mary. He died on the cross a sacrifice for our sins according to the Scriptures. Further, he arose bodily from the dead, ascended into heaven, where at the right hand of the Majesty on High, he is now our High Priest and Advocate.

4. The ministry of the Holy Spirit is to glorify the Lord Jesus Christ, and during this age, to convict men and women, regenerate the believing sinner, and indwell, guide, instruct, and empower the believer for godly living and service.

5. That mankind was created in the image of God but fell into sin and is, therefore, lost, and only through regeneration by the Holy Spirit can salvation and spiritual life be obtained.

6. That the shed blood of Jesus Christ and his resurrection provide the only ground for justification and salvation for all who believe, and only such as receive Jesus Christ are born of the Holy Spirit and, thus, become children of God.

7. In the bodily resurrection of the dead; of the believer to everlasting blessedness and joy with the Lord; of the unbeliever to judgment and everlasting conscious punishment.

Theological Principles

A. We are committed to the Great Commandment and believe the way we can best love God with all our being is to obey him with all that we are; heart, soul, and mind (Matt. 22:36–38). The best application is to fully obey the Great Commission, first by being a disciple, and then by making disciples. Among leaders, this calls for leading the church to be a Great Commandment, Great Commission church (Matt. 28:18–20).

B. The mission must come first (Luke 9:23–25). By placing the mission first, there is impact in the community harvest field and the members' spiritual needs are met. The church is to multiply through its leaders and members. They are to actively seek to plant other churches as a means of evangelism.

C. You cannot make disciples without accountability, and you cannot develop a helpful accountability system without structure. This is the role of church leaders (Matt. 28:20; 1 Thess. 5:14).

D. There are eleven principles of disciple making that are taught in the process.

1. A disciple-making church employs an intentional strategy based on its theology of mission. A theology of mission answers both the why and how questions. Why are we here and how are we going to fulfill our mission?
2. Making disciples is the primary work and purpose of a church because it creates healthy Christians and through reproduction and multiplication the world is evangelized God's way. Thus, it meets the requirement of glorifying God to the fullest through obedience and bearing of fruit.
3. A church must properly and clearly identify the role of the pastor, the people, and the disciple-making process.
4. The priesthood of every believer. All Christians are called ministers of the gospel and are empowered and gifted to fulfill God's will for their life and their church.
5. Multiplication is both a principle and a method for increasing the impact and outreach of a congregation.

6. Apprenticeship is critical to leadership development, i.e., the church creates a system that chooses potential leaders, trains them, tests them, and then deploys them.
7. Leaders should be selected by character and by gifts, in that order.
8. Philosophical purity must be maintained at the leadership level.
9. Accountability serves as a catalyst to obedience.
10. Decentralization of ministry is possible through small groups.
11. Evangelism is a catalyst to the practice of the spiritual disciplines.

E. We believe that change is vital to any congregation's ability to be renewed and reformed. But before change can occur, values must be adjusted or clarified so that people see the need for change.

F. We believe high commitment is for the normal Christian life and that it can be built and managed. A high-commitment environment is possible within the contemporary evangelical church.

G. We believe the pastor's primary role is to prepare people for the work of ministry by being an instructor in the Christian life, teaching people to obey. This is much more than simply dispensing great truths, no matter how eloquent one might be. Preaching is the first and most important step in making disciples in the local church, but only the first step.

H. We believe that the training phases modeled by Christ are a helpful paradigm for understanding how to assist people on their spiritual journeys. While we don't see the phases as the purpose of the Gospels or a true systematic theology, we do see them as an insightful truth modeled by Jesus. Those phases are "Come and See," "Come Follow Me," "Be with Me," and "Remain in Me." These are outlined in *New Century Disciple Making*.[1]

Definition of Disciple Making

Its Scope

- Deliverance of evangelizing
- Development or training
- Deployment or mission

This represents a full-bodied philosophy that teaches that we all become disciples at the point of conversion and that we engage in discipleship and are discipled all our lives, even after we are deployed into mission. The scope is as broad as "teaching them to obey everything I commanded you" (Matt. 28:20). There are 212 commands from Christ.

Its Process

Accountability is added to the intentional training of a disciple, balancing love against biblical mandate.

Training Principles

- Leaders need hands-on help to experience transformational change. This means practical tools and advice with coaching over a long period of time.
- Leaders need ongoing coaching because developing people is a process, and you cannot teach a process with an event—you teach a process through a process. This is why the full training to produce lasting change is 1,000 days. Follow-up surveys show 50 percent of churches have finished the seven milestones (see Journey Map) by the end of two years. Adding an additional twelve months elevates the impact and completion rate for all but a few churches. About 80 percent of churches experience significant transformation, 20 percent are impacted to a lesser degree.

- Leaders need to work together in teams to break through barriers that normally impede real transformational progress. It is the "you had to be there to get it" syndrome. Many pastors struggle with convincing their leaders that such an investment of time, money, and effort is worth it. Often it is in the pastor-to-leader discussion where any real chance of change dies. This environment allows change, within three days, previously not possible through repeated effort.

- Accountability is essential for success. This is not heavy-handed or abusive accountability. It is helping people keep their commitments to God. There is built-in accountability in the process in that the team has taken the time—and the church has spent the money—so there is an expectation of tangible results. There is positive peer pressure between churches as they regularly report to others what they have accomplished. The track leader helps the team members complete their projects. Finally, all team members sign a covenant that they will give it their best. It is hard to imagine anything more positive than helping people keep their commitments to God.

- We believe that teams are better served by attending three tracks: leadership, education, and outreach. These are critical components in a vital church.

- The training should combine inspiration and skill development. For that reason, there are plenary sessions that address a theology of mission and individual tracks to coach participants through a hands-on application of principles appropriate to their context and setting. Integration of tracks and implementation of plans are also part of the track experience.

- We are committed to biblical principles before any method; training is principle driven. Churches need to write their own scripts by customizing these principles to their congregations and cultures.

229

- Leaders are instructed on how best to use the many curricula available today.
- We are committed to multiplication of our training through other like-minded church leaders around the world, called apprentices.
- We are committed to multiplication of our training through partnerships with denominations, networks, and mission organizations around the globe. We realize others carry the same vision, and we know there are kindred Spirit-filled fellow leaders who care as deeply as we do about the renewal and rescue of the church.

Appendix C

Sample Church Plan

Step One: Goal Statement

In the next twenty-four months we plan to help our church become a disciple-making church by:

1. Starting a small group ministry.
2. Beginning leadership training.
3. Developing a leadership community.

This will glorify God by making disciples who reproduce and who are equipped to minister. It will also strengthen the church by meeting the physical and spiritual needs of our members.

Step Two: Goal Stated in Measurable Quantities and Qualities

We plan to become a disciple-making church by accomplishing the following in twenty-four months.

Quantitatively

1. We will have two or more basic accountability groups meeting once a week.
2. We will have two or more covenant groups meeting once a week.
3. We will have a leadership community and an apprentice program.
4. Within the time frame specified above, we will have three or more fishing-pool projects.

Qualitatively

1. Those involved will develop a faith that is obedient and thereby increase their commitment to Scripture, to one another, to prayer, to praise and worship, and to outreach.
2. Those involved will know the joy of being the type of person God desires—a disciple who is fully trained.

Step Three: Goal Stated in Measurements and Expected Results

Measurements We Will Use

1. We will count the number and the types of groups every four months.
2. We will see how often each group is meeting and determine each group's attendance.
3. We will count the number of apprentices involved in the leadership community and the number of potential apprentice candidates every four months.
4. We will survey the people involved in the leadership community every four months to ascertain whether the leadership community is helping to educate and motivate their faith and desire.

Expected Results

1. We expect two or more basic accountability groups to be in operation by the end of the year.
2. We expect to add two or more covenant groups late this year or early next year.
3. We expect to have a leadership community that meets twice a month.
4. We expect to have an apprentice program operational at the end of the year.
5. We expect to add eight new believers to the church through the fishing-pool events.

Step Four: Goal Stated in Phases

Phase One: Start Date—January 18
Completion/Evaluation Date—May 16

Planned Actions

1. We will begin leader training using two basic accountability groups, both led by the pastor, who is already trained in small-group leadership.
2. Curriculum will be Navs 2:7 materials and small-group materials.
3. We will strongly recruit existing board members and adult Sunday school leaders as well as potential small-group leaders to attend.
4. We will meet weekly and plan to have sixteen persons involved.
5. We will prayerfully collect a list of at least six potential apprentices.
6. We will present a six-week preaching series on *The Disciple-Making Church*.

233

Measurement

By May 16 we should have

1. Two basic accountability groups meeting weekly.
2. At least sixteen persons attending.
3. At least half of the board members attending.
4. At least six potential apprentices ready to be trained.
5. Completed a six-week series on disciple making.

Phase Two: Start Date—May 16
Completion/Evaluation Date—November 11

Planned Actions

1. Continue two basic accountability groups.
2. Begin leadership community meetings (vision section only) twice a month.
3. Potential apprentices in accountability groups will begin to attend leadership community.

Measurement

By November 11 we should have

1. Sixteen persons continuing in basic accountability groups.
2. At least six of these selected as apprentices.
3. A (vision only) leadership community meeting twice a month.

Phase Three: Start Date—November 11
Completion/Evaluation Date—May 13

Planned Actions

1. Apprentices will start two covenant groups, two new basic accountability groups, one additional "congre-

234

gation," at least one fishing pool, and continue in their basic accountability group.
2. The leadership community will be expanded to include both a vision and a training section.
3. Each group leader will recruit an apprentice by the end of this phase.

Measurement

By May 13 we should have

1. Two covenant groups.
2. Four basic accountability groups.
3. One new congregation.
4. Seven apprentices.
5. A full-blown leadership community meeting twice a month.
6. One fishing pool.

Notes

Chapter 1: *What Is Revival?*

1. Robert Coleman, *The Coming World Revival* (Wheaton: Crossway, 1995), 18.

2. Iain Murray, *Revival and Revivalism* (Carlisle, Pa.: Banner of Truth), 23.

3. Richard Lovelace, *Dynamics of Spiritual Life* (Wheaton: InterVarsity, 1976), 38.

4. Murray, *Revival and Revivalism,* 374

5. Lovelace, *Dynamics of Spiritual Life,* 47.

6. Ibid., 48–49.

7. Calvin Colton, *History and Character of American Revivals of Religion* (London), 4.

8. J. H. Rice, *Memoir of Rice,* 338.

9. See Charles Finney, *Lectures on Revival* (Minneapolis: Bethany, 1988), 161–75.

10. James McLoughlin, *Modern Revivalism* (New York: Ronald Press, 1959), 97.

11. Søren Kierkegaard, *Attack upon Christendom* (Princeton, N.J.: Princeton University Press, 1944), 41.

12. Murray, *Revival and Revivalism,* 376.

13. J. I. Packer, *A Quest for Holiness* (Wheaton: Crossway, 1990), 36.

14. Ibid.

15. Ibid., 316–22.

16. Os Guinness, *The American Hour* (New York: Macmillan Free Press, 1993), 387.

Chapter 2: *Do We Need Revival?*

1. Murray, *Revival and Revivalism,* 387.

2. George Barna, *Vital Signs* (Wheaton: 1984), 9.

3. George Gallup, "The Spiritual Fitness Assessment" (paper presented in Colorado Springs, 1996).

4. Rick Warren, *The Purpose Driven Church* (Grand Rapids: Zondervan, 1996), 82.

5. Peter Drucker, *Leadership Journal* (fall 1996): 54–55.

6. Thomas C. Reeves, *The Empty Church: The Suicide of Liberal Christianity* (New York: The Free Press, 1996), 1–31.

7. James Hunter, *Evangelicalism: The Coming Generation* (Chicago: University of Chicago Press, 1987), 205.

8. Charles Trueheart, "The Next Church," *Atlantic Monthly* (August 1996): 37ff.

9. Bob Gilliam, *Evangelism Report* (Minneapolis: Evangelical Free Church of America, 1992).

10. There are a variety of reasons for such an anemic showing. I've written about many of them in *Seven Steps to Transform Your Church* (Grand Rapids: Revell, 1997). See the chapter "Evangelism."

11. Mike Regele and Mark Schulz, *Death of the Church* (Grand Rapids: Zondervan, 1996).

Chapter 3: *Breakthroughs*

1. Howard Snyder, *The Problem of Wineskins* (Downers Grove, Ill.: InterVarsity, 1976), 22.

2. George Gallup and Jim Castelli, *The People's Religion* (Old Tappan, N.J.: Macmillan, 1989).

3. Ken Sidey, "Church Growth Fine Tunes Its Formulas," *Christianity Today* (June 24, 1991).

Chapter 4: *Barriers*

1. Neil Postman, *Amusing Ourselves to Death* (New York: Penguin, 1984).

2. James Hunter, *American Evangelicalism: Conservative Religion and the Quandary of Modernity* (New Brunswick, N.J.: Rutgers University Press, 1983), 75.

3. Alister McGrath, *Evangelicalism and the Future of Christianity* (Downers Grove, Ill.: InterVarsity, 1995), 128.

4. Ibid., 129.

5. For a treatment of this subject see Bill Hull, *Building High Commitment in a Low-Commitment World* (Grand Rapids: Revell, 1996).

6. Hunter, *American Evangelicalism*, 83.

7. Loren Mead, *The Once and Future Church* (New York: The Alban Institute, 1991).

8. Joel Barker, *Future Edge* (New York: William Morrow, 1991), 140.

9. Lyle Schaller, *The New Reformation* (Nashville: Abingdon Press, 1995), 35.

10. Ibid., 33.

11. David Schmidt, *Choosing to Live: Financing the Future of Religious Bodies' Headquarters* (Milwaukee: Christian Stewardship Assoc., 1996), 28.

12. Peter Drucker, *The Effective Executive* (New York: Harper and Row, 1993).

13. Ibid., 24.

14. Schmidt, *Choosing to Live*, 93.

Chapter 5: *The Nature of Revival*

1. James Burns, *The Laws of Revival* (Minneapolis: World Wide Publications, 1993), 14.

2. Ibid., 36.

3. Henry Mitchell, "Spiritual Revival 1980s-Style," *Washington Post*, June 10, 1988, D2.

4. Hunter, *American Evangelicalism*, 133.

5. Os Guinness, *Fit Bodies, Fat Minds: Why Evangelicals Don't Think and What to Do about It* (Grand Rapids: Baker, 1994), 105 (italics mine).

6. Ibid.

7. Packer, *Quest for Holiness*, 317.

Chapter 6: *The Starting Line*

1. Packer, *Quest for Holiness*, 317.

Chapter 7: *Redefine the Mission*

1. If you desire more details than this book allows for, please call T-NET International at 1-800-995-5362.

2. Dave Travis, *Champions* 1, no. 8 (December 1996).

3. Warren, *Purpose Driven Church*, 144.

4. For greater detail, please see several of my other books, *Seven Steps to Transform Your Church* (Grand Rapids: Revell, 1997); *The Disciple-Making Pastor* (Grand Rapids: Revell, 1987); and *Building High Commitment in a Low-Commitment World* (Grand Rapids: Revell, 1996). You can also request information from T-NET International by calling 1-800-995-5362.

Chapter 8: *Redesign Your Infrastructure*

1. Jim Petersen, *Church without Walls* (Colorado Springs: NavPress, 1992), 168–70.

2. Ruben Job and Norman Shawchuck, *Guide to Prayer for Ministers and Other Servants* (Nashville: The Upper Room, 1983), 72.

3. Adapted from Mead, *The Once and Future Church*, 24.

238

4. Stephen R. Covey, *First Things First* (New York: Simon and Schuster, 1994), 89.

5. For details see Bill Hull, *The Disciple-Making Church* (Grand Rapids: Revell, 1990).

Appendix A: *New Life Church Philosophy of Ministry*

From Christian A. Schwartz, *Natural Church Development* (Carol Stream, Ill.: ChurchSmart Resources, 1996), 111.

Appendix B: *Purpose, Philosophy, and Principles*

1. Bill Hull, *New Century Disciple Making* (Grand Rapids: Revell, 1997).

Bill Hull is a pastor at Cypress Evangelical Free Church in Cypress, California. He is the former president of T-NET International and former director of Mission USA for the Evangelical Free Church of America. He is the author of *The Disciple-Making Pastor, The Disciple-Making Church, Building High Commitment in a Low-Commitment World, New Century Disciple Making, 7 Steps to Transform Your Church,* and *Revival That Reforms.*